AMERICAN BOOKSTORE
DIRECTORY

2nd Look Books
2829 E 29th Ave
Spokane WA 99223
(888) 535-6464

I0116586

32 Books and Gallery
2829 E 29th Ave
Spokane WA 99223
(888) 535-6464

57th Street Books
1301 E 57th St
Chicago IL 60637
(773) 684-1300

A Book Above
136 W Vallette St Ste 6
Elmhurst IL 60126
630-993-0133

A Cappella Books
208 Haralson Ave NE
Atlanta GA 30307
(404) 681-5128

A Children's Place
1423 NE Fremont St
Portland OR 97212
(503) 284-8294

AMERICAN BOOKSTORE
DIRECTORY

A Cultural Exchange
12624 Larchmere Blvd
Cleveland OH 44120
(216) 229-8300

A Folded Corner
Old Wagon Antique Mall
10685 Melody Dr # B
Northglenn CO 80234
(720) 366-1600

A Freethinker's Corner
652 Central Ave Ste A
Dover NH 03820
603-319-7648

A Good Book
1014 Main St
Sumner WA 98390
(253) 891-9692

A Great Good Place for Books
6120 La Salle Ave
Oakland CA 94611
(510) 339-8210

A Great Yarn
894 Main St
Chatham MA 02633
(508) 237-2053

AMERICAN BOOKSTORE
DIRECTORY

A Likely Story
7566 Main St
Sykesville MD 21784
(410) 795-1718

A Little Bookish
8898 Old Lee Hwy. Ste 110
Ooltewah TN 37363
(423) 653-1360

A New Chapter Bookstore
2824 Terrell Rd Ste 309
Greenville TX 75402
(903) 454-9199

A New Chapter Bookstore
922 Washington Street West
Lewisburg WV 24901
(423) 677-0389

A Novel Bookstore
305 1st St S # 1
Yelm WA 98597
(360) 458-4722

A Novel Experience
426 Thomaston St
Zebulon GA 30295
(770) 567-1103

AMERICAN BOOKSTORE
DIRECTORY

A Novel Idea
118 N 14th St
Lincoln NE 68508
(402) 475-8663

A Novel Idea
1726 E. Passyunk Avenue
Philadelphia PA 19148
(267) 764-1202

A Reader's Corner
2044 Frankfort Ave
Louisville KY 40206
(502) 897-5578

A Room Of One's Own Bookstore
315 W Gorham St
Madison WI 53703
(608) 257-7888

A Seat at the Table Books
9630 Bruceville Rd Suite 106-317
Elk Grove CA 95757
(510) 246-6434

Aaron's Books
35 E Main St
Lititz PA 17543
(717) 627-1990

AMERICAN BOOKSTORE
DIRECTORY

Abednego Book Shoppe
2682 E Main St
Ventura CA 93003
(805) 643-9350

Abraham Lincoln Book Shop
824 W Superior St Ste 100
Chicago IL 60642
(312) 944-3085

Absolutely Fiction Books
903 S John Redditt Dr
Lufkin TX 75904
(936) 225-4569

Acorn Books
2421 South Dupont Blvd
Smyrna DE 19977
(302) 734-9100

Acorn Naturalists
14742 Plaza Drive Suite 100
Tustin CA 92780
(714) 838-4888

Ad Astra Books
141 N Santa Fe Ave
Salina KS 67401
(785) 833-2235

AMERICAN BOOKSTORE
DIRECTORY

Adamstown Books
555 W James St
Lancaster PA 17603
(717) 290-8712

Adirondack Reader
156 Main St
Inlet NY 13360
(315) 357-2665

Adle International
818 SW 3rd Ave Ste 284
Portland OR 97204
(415) 874-5637

Adventure Bound Books
134 North Sterling Street
Morganton NC 28655
(704) 640-2220

Adventure Ink
16218 Mil Potrero #101
Pine Mountain Club CA 93222
(805) 526-8731

Adventures Underground
1391 George Washington Way
Richland WA 99354
(509) 946-9893

Aesop's Fable

AMERICAN BOOKSTORE
DIRECTORY

400 Washington Street Suite 200
Holliston MA 01746
(508) 429-2031

Aesop's Treasury Books and Games
200 W First Street Ste 199
Farmington MO 63640
(573) 915-0266

Afikomen Judaica
3042 Claremont Ave
Berkeley CA 94705
(510) 655-1977

FK Books & Records
4801 Shore Dr Ste D
Virginia Beach VA 23455
(757) 962-1996

Afro-In Books & Internet Cafe
5575 NW 7th Ave
Miami FL 33127
(305) 978-0991

Afterwords Books
441 E Vandalia St
Edwardsville IL 62025
(618) 655-0355

Ahuva Rogers

AMERICAN BOOKSTORE
DIRECTORY

17254 Lincoln Drive
Southfield MI 48076
(248) 895-7241

AIA St. Louis Bookstore
911 Washington Ave
St. Louis MO 63101
(314) 231-4252

Al's Newsstand
177 N College Ave
Fort Collins CO 80524
(970) 482-9853

Al's Old & New Book Store
360 E William
Wichita KS 67202
(316) 264-8763

Alabama Booksmith
2626 19th Pl S
Birmingham AL 35209
(205) 870-4242

Alabama State University Bookstore
1055 Tullibody Drive
Montgomery AL 36104
(334) 229-4143

Albany State University East Campus Bookstore
504 College Dr

AMERICAN BOOKSTORE
DIRECTORY

Albany GA 31705
(229) 903-3620

Albion Books
111 Debra Lane
Buffalo NY 14207
(619) 750-7061

Alexander Book Co.
50 2nd St
San Francisco CA 94105
(415) 495-2992

Alibi Bookshop
624 Marin St
Vallejo CA 94590
(510) 229-7093

All She Wrote Books
4 Otis Street Unit 1
Somerville MA 02145
(617) 756-7308

All Things Book
8105 Old Redwood Highway
Windsor CA 95492
(360) 553-8448

All Things Inspiration Giftique
1400 Veterans Memorial Highway SE Suite 140
Mableton GA 30126

AMERICAN BOOKSTORE
DIRECTORY

(678) 671-0270

Allegheny College Bookstore
520 N Main St
Meadville PA 16335
(814) 332-5369

Alley Cat Books
3036 24th St
San Francisco CA 94110
(415) 824-1761

Alomo Books
240 S Ridgewood Road
South Orange NJ 07079
(201) 674-6456

Alter Ego Comics
331 7th Ave
Marion IA 52302
(319) 373-8935

American University Campus Bookstore
4400 Mass Ave NW
Washington DC 20016
(202) 885-6300

American Writers Museum Bookstore
180 N Michigan Ave
Chicago IL 60601
(312) 374-8790

AMERICAN BOOKSTORE
DIRECTORY

Amherst Books
8 Main St
Amherst MA 01002
(413) 256-1547

Amy's Bookcase
2530 San Juan Blvd
Farmington NM 87401
(505) 327-4647

An Unlikely Story
111 South St
Plainville MA 02762
(508) 699-0244

Anderson Books
8470 Dover Dr
Roseville CA 95746
(916) 834-2222

Anderson's Bookshop
26 S La Grange Rd
La Grange IL 60525
(708) 582-6353

Anderson's Bookshop
520 Exchange Ct
Aurora IL 60504
(630) 820-0044

AMERICAN BOOKSTORE
DIRECTORY

Anderson's Bookshop
5112 Main St
Downers Grove IL 60515
(630) 963-2665

Anderson's Bookshops
123 W Jefferson Ave
Naperville IL 60540
(630) 355-2665

Anderson's Toyshop
111 W Jefferson Ave
Naperville IL 60540
(630) 355-2665

Andersons Larchmont
96 - 98 Chatsworth Avenue
Larchmont NY 10538
(914) 834-6900

Andover Bookstore
74 Main St
Andover MA 01810
(978) 475-0143

Angel Wings Bookstore
1085 Roberts Chapel Rd
Stem NC 27581
(919) 764-0223

Angelo State University Bookstore

AMERICAN BOOKSTORE
DIRECTORY

2601 West Ave N
San Angelo TX 76909
(325) 942-2335

Anime Castle
77 Searing Ave
Mineola NY 11501
(516) 214-4484

Annie Bloom's Books
7834 SW Capitol Hwy
Portland OR 97219
(503) 245-1831

Annie's Book Stop
1330 Union Ave
Laconia NH 03246
(603) 528-4445

Annie's Book Stop
3 Man Mar Dr
Plainville MA 02762
(508) 695-2396

Another Look Books
22263 Goddard Rd
Taylor MI 48180
(734) 374-5665

Another Read Through
3932 N Mississippi Ave

AMERICAN BOOKSTORE
DIRECTORY

Portland OR 97227
(503) 208-2729

Another Story Bookshop
315 Roncesvalles Ave
Toronto ON M6R2M6
(416) 462-1104

ANT Bookstore
345 Clifton Ave
Clifton NJ 07011
(973) 777-2704

Anticus
7012 E Greenway Pkwy Suite #160
Scottsdale AZ 85254
(480) 695-0409

Antigone Books
411 N 4th Ave
Tucson AZ 85705
(520) 792-3715

Apostle Islands Booksellers
112 Rittenhouse Ave
Bayfield WI 54814
(715) 779-0200

Appalachian State University Book Store
219 College St
Boone NC 28608

AMERICAN BOOKSTORE
DIRECTORY

(828) 262-3072

Appletree Books
12419 Cedar Rd
Cleveland Heights OH 44106
(216) 791-2665

Arcade Booksellers
15 Purchase St
Rye NY 10580
(914) 967-0966

Arcadia Books
102 E Jefferson St
Spring Green WI 53588
(608) 588-7638

Arcana: Books on the Arts
8675 Washington Blvd
Culver City CA 90232
(310) 458-1499

Archestratus Books
160 Huron St
Brooklyn NY 11222
(718) 349-7711

Archives Book Shop
517 W Grand River Ave
East Lansing MI 48823
(517) 332-8444

AMERICAN BOOKSTORE
DIRECTORY

Argos Book Shop
1405 Robinson Rd SE
Grand Rapids MI 49506
(616) 454-0111

Art of STEM Books
7425 N Leavitt Ave
Portland OR 97203
(503) 206-6214

Arte of The Booke
2401 Windsor Ave SW
Roanoke VA 24015
(540) 342-0738

Artifact Books
603 S. Coast Hwy 101
Encinitas CA 92024
(760) 436-7892

Arts & Letters Bookstore
113 E Bridge St
Granbury TX 76048
(817) 229-8511

Arundel Books
212 1st Ave S
Seattle WA 98104
(206) 624-4442
Asia Fine Books

AMERICAN BOOKSTORE
DIRECTORY

1016 Cherry Ave
Charlottesville VA 22903
(434) 293-7379

Asia Store
725 Park Ave
New York NY 10021
(212) 327-9309

Asian Art Museum
200 Larkin St
San Francisco CA 94102
(415) 581-3607

Astoria Bookshop
31-29 31st Street
Astoria NY 11106
(718) 278-2665

ASU Bookstore
525 E Orange St
Tempe AZ 85287
(480) 965-3191

ASUN Bookstore
87 W Stadium Way/J Crowley Student Union
Reno NV 89557
(775) 784-6597

Atlanta History Center Shop
130 W Paces Ferry Rd

AMERICAN BOOKSTORE
DIRECTORY

Atlanta GA 30305
(404) 814-4114

Atlanta Vintage Books
3660 Clairmont Road
Atlanta GA 30341
(770) 457-2919

Atomic Books
3620 Falls Rd
Baltimore MD 21211
(410) 662-4444

Atticus Books
738 Lower Main Street
Park City UT 84060
(435) 214-7241

Auburn University Bookstore
1360 Haley Center
Auburn AL 36849
(334) 844-1365

Auntie's Bookstore
402 W Main Ave
Spokane WA 99201
(509) 838-0206

Austy's
503 Florence Street
Salem IN 47167

AMERICAN BOOKSTORE
DIRECTORY

(812) 570-0258

Author's Books SJC TA-23 (1793)
Mineta San Jose Int'l - Hudson News
San Jose CA 95131
(408) 441-2635

Author's Bookstore MSP C67 (2595)
WDFG
St. Paul MN 55432
(612) 499-4357

Author's Bookstore ONT T2-210 (1870)
WDFG 2900 E. Airport Drive Suite 2365 Ontario
CA 91761
(909) 214-8996

Ave Maria Community
1084 S De Anza Blvd
San Jose CA 95129
(408) 725-1511

Avid Bookshop
493 Prince Ave
Athens GA 30601
(706) 352-2060

Avid Bookshop Five Points
1662 S Lumpkin St
Athens GA 30606
(706) 850.2843

AMERICAN BOOKSTORE
DIRECTORY

Avid Reader Active
605 2nd St
Davis CA 95616
(530) 759-1599

Avoid The Day Bookstore
211 Beach 90th Street
Rockaway Beach NY11693
(860) 944-4847

Away With Words Bookshop
18954 Front St NE Suite 100
Poulsbo WA 98370
(360) 932-5547

B & B Booksellers
278 Main St
Chester CA 96020
(530) 258-2150

Babar Books
46 Rue Ste. Anne #6
Pointe-Claire QC H9S 4P8
(514) 694-0380

Babycake's Book Stack
291 7th St W Apt 1502
St. Paul MN 55102
(651) 428-7118

AMERICAN BOOKSTORE
DIRECTORY

Bacchus & Books
10 Gillon Street
Charleston SC 29401
(703) 599-024

Back of Beyond Books
83 N Main St
Moab UT 84532
(435) 259-5154

Badger's Bookshop
4730 Cooper Ave
Lincoln NE 68506
(402) 314-6602

Baker Book House
2768 East Paris Ave SE
Grand Rapids MI 49546
(616) 957-3110

Baldwin's Book Barn
865 Lenape Rd
West Chester PA 19382
(610) 696-0816

Ballast Book Co
409 Pacific Ave #202
Bremerton WA 98337
(360) 626-3430

Baltimore Read Aloud

AMERICAN BOOKSTORE
DIRECTORY

919 W 34th Street #50215
Baltimore MD 21211
(443) 714-3455

Bank of Books
748 E Main St
Ventura CA 93001
(805) 643-3154

Bank Square Books
53 W Main St
Mystic CT 06355
(860) 536-3795

Bank Street Bookstore
2780 Broadway
New York NY 10025
(212) 678-1654

Banyen Books and Sound
3608 West 4th Avenue
Vancouver BC V6R 1P1
(604) 629-2190

Barbara Galvin
318 Nutt St
Wilmington NC 28401
(910) 762-4444

Barbara's Bestsellers at Boston South Station
700 Atlantic Ave

AMERICAN BOOKSTORE
DIRECTORY

Boston MA 02110
(617) 443-0060

Barbara's Bookstore
201 E Huron St
Chicago IL 60611
(312) 926-2665

Barbara's Bookstore
111 N State St Lower Level
Chicago IL 60602
(312) 666-3178

Barbara's Bookstore
810 Village Center Dr
Burr Ridge IL 60527
(630) 920-1500

Barbara's Bookstore
Hawthorn Mall
Vernon Hills IL 60061
(847) 549-7550

Barbara's Bookstore
85 Arroyo Hondo Rd
Santa Fe NM 87508
(505) 988-4881

Barbara's Bookstore
111 North State Street
Chicago IL 60602

AMERICAN BOOKSTORE
DIRECTORY

(312) 781-5257

Barbara's Bookstore
2651 Navy Blvd
Glenview IL 60026
(847) 904-7304

Barbara's Bookstore ORD T1 B10 (841)
Chicago O'Hare - Barbara's Books
Chicago IL 60666
(773) 686-1281

Barbara's Bookstore ORD T2 E3 (842)
Chicago O'Hare - Barbara's Books
Chicago IL 60666
(773) 686-1281

Barbara's Bookstore ORD T3 G1 (840)
Chicago O'Hare - Barbara's Books
Chicago IL 60666
(773) 686-1281

Barbara's Bookstore ORD T3 K5 (845)
Chicago O'Hare - Barbara's Books
Chicago IL 60666
(773) 686-1281

Barbara's Bookstore ORD T3 L1 (839)
Chicago O'Hare - Barbara's Books
Chicago IL 60666
(773) 686-1281

AMERICAN BOOKSTORE
DIRECTORY

Barbed Wire Books
504 Main St Unit A
Longmont CO 80501
(303) 827-3620

Bards Alley
110 Church St NW
Vienna VA 22180
(703) 863-4484

Barjon's Books
221 N 29th St
Billings MT 59101
(406) 252-4398

Barn Owl Books
373 Main St
Quincy CA 95971
(530) 283-2665

Barn Owl Books
373 Main Street
Quincy CA 95971
(530) 283-2665

Barrett Bookstore
6 Corbin Dr
Darien CT 06820
(203) 655-2712

AMERICAN BOOKSTORE
DIRECTORY

Barrington Books
184 County Rd
Barrington RI 02806
(401) 245-7925

Barrington Books Retold
176 Hillside Rd
Cranston RI 02920
(401) 432-7222

Barron's of Texas
405 W Loop 281
Longview TX 75605
(903) 663-2060

Barstons Child's Play
5536 Connecticut Ave NW
Washington DC 20015
(202) 244-3602

Barstons Child's Play
4510 Lee Hwy
Arlington VA 22207
(703) 522-1022

Barstons Child's Play
1382 Chain Bridge Rd
McLean VA 22101
(703) 448-3444

Barstons Child's Play

AMERICAN BOOKSTORE
DIRECTORY

1661 Rockville Pike
Rockville MD 20852
(301) 230-9040

Bart's Books
306 W Matlija St
Ojai CA 93023
(805) 646-3755

Bartleby's Books
17 W Main Street
Wilmington VT 05363
(802) 464-5425

Basically Books
1672 Kamehameha Ave
Hilo HI 96720
(808) 961-0144

Basile History Market
450 W Ohio St
Indianapolis IN 46202
(317) 234-3683

Bates College Store
56 Campus Ave
Lewiston ME 04240
(207) 786-6121

Battenkill Books
15 E Main St

AMERICAN BOOKSTORE
DIRECTORY

Cambridge NY 12816
(518) 677-2515

Battery Park Book Exchange
1 Page Ave
Asheville NC 28801
(828) 252-0020

Bay Books
131 Main St
St. Louis MS 39520
(228) 463-2688

Bay Books
419 N. St. Joseph Street
Suttons Bay MI 49682
(616) 822-6918

Bay Books
1029 Orange Ave
Coronado CA 92118
(619) 435-0070

Bay Tree Bookstore
University Of California
Santa Cruz CA 95064
(831) 459-4544

Baylor Bookstore
1201 S 5th St
Waco TX 76706

AMERICAN BOOKSTORE
DIRECTORY

(254) 710-2161

Bayou Book Company
1118 John Sims Pkwy E
Niceville FL 32578
(850) 678-1593

BayShore Books
302 Collins Ave
Oconto WI 54153
(920) 834-3220

Bayswater Book Company
23 Main St Center
Harbor NH 03226
(603) 253-8858

Bbgb books
3003 W Cary St
Richmond VA 23221
(804) 353-5675

Beach Books
616 Broadway St
Seaside OR 97138
(503) 738-3500

Beagle and Wolf Books & Bindery
112 3rd St W
Park Rapids MN 56470
(218) 237-2665

AMERICAN BOOKSTORE
DIRECTORY

Beanbag Books
25 W Winter St
Delaware OH 43015
(740) 363-0290

Beanbag Books
25 W Winter St
Delaware OH 43015
(740) 363-0290

Bear Pond Books
77 Main St
Montpelier VT 05602
(802) 229-0774

Bear Pond Books
38 Main Street
Stowe VT 05672
(802) 253-8236

Beaverdale Books
2629 Beaver Ave
Des Moines IA 50310
(515) 279-5400

Bee Hive Books
328 Montezuma Ave
Santa Fe NM 87501
(505) 780-8051

AMERICAN BOOKSTORE
DIRECTORY

Beers Book Center
915 S St
Sacramento CA 95811
(916) 442-9475

Bel and Bunna's Books
3581 Mt Diablo Blvd Ste C
Lafayette CA 94549
(925) 298-5512

Bell's Book Store
536 Emerson St
Palo Alto CA 94301
(650) 323-7822

Belmont Books
79 Leonard St
Belmont MA 02478
(617) 932-1496

Bergen Community College Bookstore
400 Paramus Rd
Paramus NJ 07652
(201) 445-7174

Berkeley Art Museum Store
2625 Durant Ave
Berkeley CA 94720
(510) 642-0808

Berry & Co.

AMERICAN BOOKSTORE
DIRECTORY

51 Division St.
Sag Harbor NY 11963
(631) 539-1791

Best of Books
1313 E Danforth Rd
Edmond OK 73034
(405) 340-9202

Bestsellers Books & Coffee Co.
360 S Jefferson St
Mason MI 48854
(517) 676-6648

Bethany Beach Books
99 Garfield Pkwy
Bethany Beach DE 19930
(302) 539-2522

Bethune-Cookman University Bookstore
740 W International Speedway
Daytona Beach FL 32114
(386) 481-2145

Better World Books
55740 Currant RD
Mishawaka IN 46545
(888) 510-7103

AMERICAN BOOKSTORE
DIRECTORY

Betty's Books
1813 Main St
Baker City OR 97814
(541) 523-7551

Between Books 2.0
2115 Marsh Road
Arden DE 19810
(302) 798-3111

Between the Covers
106 E Main St
Harbor Springs MI 49740
(231) 526-6658

Between the Covers
224 W Colorado Ave
Telluride CO 81435
(970) 728-4504

Between the Lines Bookstore
2549 Colonial Way
Zachary LA 70791
(225) 389-6392

Bexter Book & Copy
105 2nd Ave SW
Milaca MN 56353
(320) 983-3787

Beyond Barcodes Bookstore

108 N Main St Ste B
Kokomo IN 46901
(765) 271-5537

Bibliobar
5435 N. Garland Ave #140-544
Garland TX 75040
(214) 287-5237

Biblion Books
205 2nd St
Lewes DE 19958
(302) 644-2210

Big Blue Marble Bookstore
551 Carpenter Ln
Philadelphia PA 19119
(215) 844-1870

Big Elephant Books
4022 Honor Circle
Chattanooga TN 37416
(423) 645-8393

Big Planet Comics of Washington DC
1520 U St NW
Washington DC 20009
(202) 342-1961

Bilingual Resources
2 Walworth Ave

AMERICAN BOOKSTORE
DIRECTORY

Scarsdale NY 10583
(617) 642-5518

Binnacle Books
321 Main St
Beacon NY 12508
(718) 288-6759

Biola University Bookstore
13800 Biola Avenue
La Mirada CA 90639
(562) 903-4883

Birchbark Books & Native Arts
2115 W 21st St
Minneapolis MN 55405
(612) 374-4023

Birchbark Books and Gifts
11 First Avenue W
Grand Marais MN 55604
(218) 387-2315

Bird & Beckett Books & Records
653 Chenery St
San Francisco CA 94131
(415) 586-3733

Bird in Hand
11 E 33rd St
Baltimore MD 21218

AMERICAN BOOKSTORE
DIRECTORY

(410) 243-0757

Bisbee Books & Music
2 Copper Queen Plaza
Bisbee AZ 85603
(630) 452-3293

Black Bird Bookstore
4033 Judah St
San Francisco CA 94122
(628) 256-0081

Black Bond Books #3
Haney Place Mall
Maple Ridge V2X 8R9
(604) 463-8624

Black Bond Books #4
Semiahmoo Shopping Center
White Rock V4A 4N3
(604) 636-3336

Black Bond Books #5
Junction Shopping Centre
Mission V2V 6M7
(604) 814-2650

Black Bond Books #6
Tenant Park Square Shopping Center
Ladner V4K 1W4
(604) 946-6677

AMERICAN BOOKSTORE
DIRECTORY

Black Bond Books #7
Central City Mall
Surrey BC V3T 2W1
(604) 583-1282

Black Dog Books
188 Spring St
Newton NJ 07860
(201) 230-3900

Blair Books & More
58 The Common
Chester VT 05143
(802) 875-3400

Bliss Books & Bindery
120 E. 9th Ave Suite #1
Stillwater OK 74074
(405) 332-5653

Bloomsburg University Store
400 E 2nd St
Bloomsburg PA 17815
(570) 389-4175

Bloomsbury Books
290 E Main Street
Ashland OR 97520
(541) 488-0029

AMERICAN BOOKSTORE
DIRECTORY

Blue Bicycle Books
420 King St
Charleston SC 29403
(843) 722-2666

Blue Cypress Books
8126 Oak St
New Orleans LA 70118
(504) 352-0096

Blue Door Books
501A Central Ave
Cedarhurst NY 11516
(516) 837-0040

Blue Hill Books
26 Pleasant St
Blue Hill ME 04614
(207) 374-5632

Blue House Books
624 57th St
Kenosha WI 53142
(262) 484-1776

Blue Marble Books
1356 S Fort Thomas Ave
Fort Thomas KY 41075
(859) 781-0602

Blue Moon Antique Mall and Bookstore

AMERICAN BOOKSTORE
DIRECTORY

8230 Thomas Nelson Hwy
Lovingston VA 22949
(434) 263-8890

Blue Ridge Books
428 Hazelwood Ave
Waynesville NC 28786
(828) 456-6000

Blue Willow Bookshop
14532 Memorial Dr
Houston TX 77079
(281) 497-8675

Bluebird Books
2 S Main St
Hutchinson KS 67501
(620) 259-6868

Bluestocking Books
3817 5th Ave
San Diego CA 92103
(619) 296-1424

Bluestockings Books
172 Allen St
New York NY 10002
(212) 777-6028

Bob's Beach Books
1735 NW Highway 101

AMERICAN BOOKSTORE
DIRECTORY

Lincoln City OR 97367
(541) 994-4467

Bodacious Bookstore & Cafe
110 E. Intendencia St.
Pensacola FL 32502
(850) 934-8444

Bodhi Tree Bookstore
956 Lake St Ste A
Venice CA 90291
(310) 399-0815

Body Mind & Soul Books
7951 Katy Freeway Ste N
Houston TX 77024
(713) 993-0550

Bogan Books
130 West Main Street
Fort Kent ME 04743
(207) 231-0078

Bolen Books
111-1644 Hillside Avenue
Victoria BC V8T2C5
(250) 595-4232

Boneshaker Books
2002 23rd Ave S
Minneapolis MN 55404

AMERICAN BOOKSTORE
DIRECTORY

(612) 871-7110

Bonjour Books DC
3758 Howard Ave
Kensington MD 20895
(240) 383-9163

Book & Game Company
38 E Main St
Walla Walla WA 99362
(509) 529-9963

Book 'n' Brush
518 N Market Blvd
Chehalis WA 98532
(360) 748-6221

Book and Puppet Company
466 Northampton Street
Easton PA 18042
(484) 541-5379

Book Beat
26010 Greenfield Rd
Oak Park MI 48237
(248) 968-1190

Book Bin
1151 Church St
Northbrook IL 60062
(847) 498-4999

AMERICAN BOOKSTORE
DIRECTORY

Book Bin
25304 Lankford Highway
Onley VA 23418
(757) 787-7866

Book Carnival
348 S Tustin St
Orange CA 92866
(714) 538-3210

Book City
348 Danforth Avenue
Toronto ON M4K 1P1
(416) 469-9997

Book Club
197 East 3rd Street
New York NY 10009
(262) 227-0015

Book Culture
536 W 112th St
New York NY 10025
(212) 865-1588

Book Culture
26-09 Jackson Ave
Long Island City NY 11101
(718) 440-3120

AMERICAN BOOKSTORE
DIRECTORY

Book Culture
2915 Broadway
New York NY 10025
(646) 403-3000

Book Culture
450 Columbus Ave
New York NY 10024
(212) 595-1962

Book Ends
559 Main St
Winchester MA 01890
(781) 721-5933

Book Exchange
2932 Canton Rd
Marietta GA 30066
(770) 427-4848

Book Haven
109 North F St
Salida CO 81201
(719) 539-9629

Book Heads
216 E Mill St
Plymouth WI 53073
(920) 892-6657

Book House of Stuyvesant Plaza

AMERICAN BOOKSTORE
DIRECTORY

1475 Western Ave
Albany NY 12203
(518) 489-4761

Book Larder
4252 Fremont Ave N
Seattle WA 98103
(206) 397-4271

Book Mart & Cafe
120 E Main St
Starkville MS 39759
(662) 323-2844

Book Mine
522 Harrison Ave
Leadville CO 80461
(719) 486-2866

Book Moon
86 Cottage St
Easthampton MA 01027
(413) 203-1636

Book No Further
112 Market St SE
Roanoke VA 24011
(540) 206-2505

Book Passage
51 Tamal Vista Blvd

AMERICAN BOOKSTORE
DIRECTORY

Corte Madera CA 94925
(415) 927-0960

Book Passage
1 Ferry Building Ste 42
San Francisco CA 94111
(415) 835-1020

Book People
2923 Hamilton Blvd
Sioux City IA 51104
(712) 258-1471

Book People
536 Granite Ave
Richmond VA 23226
(804) 288-4346

Book Revue
313 New York Ave
Huntington NY 11743
(631) 271-1442

Book Show
1993 Blake Ave
Los Angeles CA 90039
(818) 522-6236

Book Soup
8818 W Sunset Blvd
West Hollywood CA 90069

AMERICAN BOOKSTORE
DIRECTORY

(310) 659-3110

Book Soup LAX (1432)
Los Angeles Int'l - Hudson News
Carson CA 90746
(310) 338-2053

Book Soup LAX T7 (1475)
Los Angeles Int'l - Hudson News
Carson CA 90746
(310) 338-2053

Book Stop
603 South Military Avenue
Green Bay WI 54303
(920)498-0008

Book Suey
10345 Joseph Campau Ave
Hamtramck MI 48212
(313) 398-2017

Book Universe
1280 Mill St
Eugene OR 97401
(541) 484-2815

Book Vault
105 S. Market
Oskaloosa IA 52577
(641) 676-1777

AMERICAN BOOKSTORE
DIRECTORY

Book-A-Holic
8760 W 21st N Suite 108
Wichita KS 67218
(316) 721-5575

BookBar
4280 Tennyson St
Denver CO 80212
(720) 443-2227

Bookbinders Basalt
760 E Valley Rd Ste C-122
Basalt CO 81621
(970) 279-5040

Bookbook
266 Bleecker St
New York NY 10014
(212) 807-8655

Bookbound
1729 Plymouth Rd
Ann Arbor MI 48105
(734) 369-4345

Bookbrokers
3200 S Airport Rd #426
Traverse City MI 49684
(231) 943-1707

AMERICAN BOOKSTORE
DIRECTORY

Bookbug
3019 Oakland Dr
Kalamazoo MI 49008
(269) 385-2847

Bookburgh Books
60 Smithfield Blvd
Plattsburgh NY 12901
(518) 566-4323

Booked
506 Main St.
Evanston IL 60202
(847) 701-5707

Bookends & Beginnings
1712 Sherman Ave Rear 1
Evanston IL 60201
(224) 999-7722

BookEnds
600 Kailua Rd
Kailua HI 96734
(808) 261-1996

Bookends
211 E Ridgewood Ave
Ridgewood NJ 07450
(201) 445-0726

Bookends On Main

AMERICAN BOOKSTORE
DIRECTORY

214 Main St E
Menomonie WI 54751
(715) 233-6252

BookHampton
41 Main St
East Hampton NY 11937
(631) 324-4939

Bookie's
10324 S Western Avenue
Chicago IL 60643
(773) 239-1110

Bookie's
2015 Ridge Road
Homewood IL 60430
(708) 377-0789

BookLink Booksellers Inc.
150 Main St Thornes Marketplace
Northampton MA 01060
(413) 585-9955

BookLore Stores
121 First Street
Orangeville ON L9W 3J8
(519) 942-3830

Booklovers Gourmet
55 E Main St

AMERICAN BOOKSTORE
DIRECTORY

Webster MA 01570
(508) 949-6232

Bookmans
6230 E. Speedway Blvd.
Tucson AZ 85712
(520) 748-9555

Bookmans
1520 S Riordan Ranch St
Flagstaff AZ 86001
(520) 774-0005

Bookmans
1056 S Country Club Dr
Mesa AZ 85210
(480) 835-0505

Bookmans
3330 E. Speedway Blvd.
Tucson AZ 85716
(520) 325-5767

Bookmans
8034 N. 19th Ave.
Phoenix AZ 85021
(602) 433-0255

Bookmans Entertainment Exchange - Northwest
3733 W Ina Rd
Tucson AZ 85741

AMERICAN BOOKSTORE
DIRECTORY

(520) 881-1744

Bookmarc's
3302 Clarksville St
La Porte TX 77571
(281) 479-0596

Bookmark Booksellers Inc.
172 Queen St
Charlottetown PE C1A 4B5
(902) 566-4888

Bookmarks
634 W 4th Ste 110
Winston-Salem NC 27101
(336) 747-1471

Bookmiser
3822 Roswell Road Ste 117
Marietta GA 30062
(770) 993-1555

BookMonster
212 Santa Monica Blvd
Santa Monica CA 90401
(424) 238-8576

Bookoff Hawaii
1450 Ala Moana Blvd Ste 2250
Honolulu HI 96814
(808) 952-9115

AMERICAN BOOKSTORE
DIRECTORY

BookPal
18101 Von Karman Ave Ste 120
Irvine CA 92612
(866) 522-6657

BookPeople
603 N Lamar Blvd
Austin TX 78703
(512) 472-5050

BookPeople of Moscow
521 S Main St
Moscow ID 83843
(208) 882-2669

Books & Books
265 Aragon Ave
Coral Gables FL 33134
(305) 442-4408

Books & Books
3409 Main Highway
Coconut Grove FL 33133
(305) 477-0866

Books & Books
9700 Collins Ave
Bal Harbour FL 33154
(305) 864-4241

AMERICAN BOOKSTORE
DIRECTORY

Books & Books - Miami International Airport
2100 NW 42nd Avenue
Miami FL 33126
(786) 641-6149

Books & Books
533 Eaton St
Key West FL 33040
(305) 296-0458

Books & Books
927 Lincoln Rd
Miami Beach FL 33139
(305) 532-3222

Books & Company
1039 Summit Ave
Oconomowoc WI 53066
(262) 567-0106

Books & Mortar
955 Cherry St SE
Grand Rapids MI 49506
(616) 214-8233

Books & Mortar
955 Cherry St SE
Grand Rapids MI 49506
(616) 214-8233

Books 'N' More

AMERICAN BOOKSTORE
DIRECTORY

574 Hale Rd
Wilmington OH 45177
(937) 383-7323

Books and Cookies
2230 Main St
Santa Monica CA 90405
(424) 238-5299

Books and Crannies
50 E. Church Street Suite 4
Martinsville VA 24112
(276) 790-2481

Books and Greetings
271 Livingston St Ste G
Northvale NJ 07647
(201) 784-2665

Books and Other Found Things
13 Loudoun St SW
Leesburg VA 20175
(703) 609-7504

Books Are Magic
225 Smith St
Brooklyn NY 11231
(718) 246-BOOK

Books By The Bay
1875 Sherman Ave

AMERICAN BOOKSTORE
DIRECTORY

North Bend OR 97459
(541) 756-1215

Books By The Sea
1600 Falmouth Rd
Centerville MA 02632
(508) 771-9100

Books Connection
31208 Five Mile
Livonia MI 48154
(734) 524-1163

Books Etcetera
2340 Sudderth Dr
Ruidoso NM 88345
(575) 257-1594

Books for Less
935 N Point Dr
Alpharetta GA 30022
(770) 978-1770

BOOKS
124 N Pinon Dr
Cortez CO 81321
(970) 565-2503

Books Inc.
1501 Vermont St
San Francisco CA 94107

AMERICAN BOOKSTORE
DIRECTORY

(415) 643-3400

Books Inc.
1875 S. Bascom Ave.
Campbell CA 95008
(408) 378-2726

Books Inc.
1344 Park St
Alameda CA 94501
(510) 522-2226

Books Inc.
1491 Shattuck Ave
Berkeley CA 94704
(510) 525-7777

Books Inc.
3515 California St
San Francisco CA 94118
(415) 221-3666

Books Inc.
317 Castro St
Mountain View CA 94041
(650) 428-1234

Books Inc.
601 Van Ness Ave
San Francisco CA 94102
(415) 776-1111

AMERICAN BOOKSTORE DIRECTORY

Books Inc.
855 El Camino Real
Palo Alto CA 94301
(650) 321-0600

Books Inc.
2251 Chestnut St
San Francisco CA 94123
(415) 931-3633

Books
528 E Garfield Rd
Aurora OH 44202
(330) 995-3228

Books of Wonder
18 W 18th Street
New York NY 10011
(212) 989-3270

Books of Wonder
217 W 84th St
New York NY 10024
(212) 989-1804

Books on B
1014 B Street
Hayward CA 94541
(510) 538-3943

AMERICAN BOOKSTORE
DIRECTORY

Books on Broad
944 Broad St
Camden SC 29020
(803) 713-7323

Books on Broadway
12 1/2 W Broadway
Williston ND 58801
(701) 572-1433

Books on Call NYC
520 8th Ave Ste 320
New York NY 10018
(917) 685-9027

Books On First
202 W 1st St
Dixon IL 61021
(815) 285-2665

Books On Main
416 Main St
Murphys CA 95247
(209) 822-0681

Books on the Common
404 Main St
Ridgefield CT 06877
(203) 431-9100

Books on the Pond

AMERICAN BOOKSTORE
DIRECTORY

2144 Schoolhouse Road
Charlestown RI 02813
(914) 450-9598

Books on the Square
471 Angell St
Providence RI 02906
(401) 331-9097

Books on the Transit
28 Walter Ave
New Market ON L3Y 2T3
(416) 629-6222

Books Tell You Why
1283 Heron Nest Ct
Columbus OH 43240
(843) 849-0283

Books To Be Red
34 School Rd
Ocracoke NC 27960
(252) 928-3936

Books Unlimited
60 E. Main St
Franklin NC 28734
(828) 369-7942

Books Upstairs
126 S Chestnut St

AMERICAN BOOKSTORE
DIRECTORY

Bath PA 18014
(610) 751-9178

Books With a Past
2465 Route 97
Glenwood MD 21738
(410) 489-2705

Books with a Past at Historic Savage Mill
8600 Foundry St
Savage MD 20763
(443) 753-3131

Books Beads and More
8324 Bell Creek Rd Ste 100
Mechanicsville VA 23116
(804) 730-2665

Bookshop Benicia
636 1st St
Benicia CA 94510
(707) 747-5155

Bookshop Santa Cruz
1520 Pacific Ave
Santa Cruz CA 95060
(831) 423-0900

Bookshop West
80 W Portal Ave
San Francisco CA 94127

AMERICAN BOOKSTORE
DIRECTORY

(415) 564-8080

BookSmart
421 Vineyard Town Center
Morgan Hill CA 95037
(408) 778-6467

BookStacks
71 Main St
Bucksport ME 04416
(207) 469-8992

Bookstore 1
12 S Palm Ave
Sarasota FL 34236
(941) 365-7900

Booksy Galore
67 Westchester Ave
Pound Ridge NY 10576
(646) 285-1265

BookTowne
171 Main St
Manasquan NJ 08736
(732) 722-7255

Booktrader
2421 Nottingham Way
Hamilton NJ 08619
(609) 890-1455

AMERICAN BOOKSTORE
DIRECTORY

BookWoman
5501 N Lamar Blvd
Austin TX 78751
(512) 472-2785

Bookworks
4022 Rio Grande Blvd NW
Albuquerque NM 87107
(505) 344-8139

Bookworks
244 Spokane Ave
Whitefish MT 59937
(406) 862-4980

Bookworm
295 Main St
Edwards CO 81632
(970) 926-7323

Bookworm Surf City
1509 Long Beach Blvd
Long Beach Township NJ 08008
(609) 494-8112

Bookworm
731 N Columbia Center Blvd Ste 102
Kennewick WA 99336
(509) 735-9016

AMERICAN BOOKSTORE
DIRECTORY

Booky Joint
437 Old Mammoth Rd
Mammoth Lakes CA 93546
(760) 934-5023

Boomerang Bookshop
1103 Glenwood Ave
Greensboro NC 27403
(336) 695-2523

Boston College Bookstore
McElroy Commons
Chestnut Hill MA 02467
(800) 978-0978

Boston Tea Room
195 W 9 Mile Rd Ste B2
Ferndale MI 48220
(248) 548-1415

Boswell Book Company
2559 N Downer Ave
Milwaukee WI 53211
(414) 332-1181

Boswell's Books
10 Bridge St
Shelburne Falls MA 01370
(413) 625-9362

Boulder Book Store

AMERICAN BOOKSTORE
DIRECTORY

1107 Pearl St
Boulder CO 80302
(303) 447-2074

Boulevard Books & Cafe
7518 13th Ave
Brooklyn NY 11228
(718) 680-5881

Bound Booksellers
158 Front St Ste 106
Franklin TN 37064
(615) 656-5345

Bound To Stay Bound Books
1880 W Morton Ave
Jacksonville IL 62650
(217) 245-5191

Bound2Please Books
132 W. Main St.
Orange VA 22960
(540) 672-4000

Bowlin's Mesilla Book Center
2360 Calle Principal
Mesilla NM 88046
(575) 526-6220

Boxcar & Caboose
394 Railroad St Unit 2

AMERICAN BOOKSTORE DIRECTORY

St. Johnsbury VT 05819
(802) 748-3551

BR Books
1933 Fruitville Pike
Lancaster PA 17601
(717) 581-5887

Brace Books & More
2205 N 14th St
Ponca City OK 74601
(580) 765-5173

Bradley's Book Outlet
390 Fountain Street
Pittsburgh PA 15238
(412) 435-0015

Bradley's Book Outlet
5580 Goods Ln
Altoona PA 16620
(814) 944-2201

Bradley's Book Outlet
Cranberry Mall
Cranberry PA 16319
(814) 676-3000

Bradley's Book Outlet
5522 Shaffer Rd
DuBois PA 15801

AMERICAN BOOKSTORE
DIRECTORY

(814) 371-7500

Bradley's Book Outlet
1911 Leesburg-Grove City Rd.
Grove City PA 16127
(724) 748-3939

Bradley's Book Outlet
2334 Oakland Ave
Indiana PA 15701
(724) 349-7000

Bradley's Book Outlet
2901 East College Ave
State College PA 16801
(814) 826-2086

Bradley's Book Outlet
Galleria at Pittsburgh Mills
Tarentum PA 15084
(724) 895-3634

Bradley's Book Outlet
The Shops at Station Square
Pittsburgh PA 15219
(412) 391-3987

Bradley's Book Outlet
2019 Penn Ave
Pittsburgh PA 15222
(412) 281-3014

AMERICAN BOOKSTORE
DIRECTORY

Bradley's Book Outlet
1368 Mall Run Rd
Uniontown PA 15401
(724) 437-1919

Brancamp Books
PO Box 127
Napoleon IN 47034
(812) 756-0739

Branches Books & Gifts
40044 Highway 49 Ste B-1
Oakhurst CA 93644
(559) 641-2019

Brave + Kind Bookshop
722 W. College Ave
Decatur GA 30030
(678) 612-9688

Bravo's Book Nook at the Players Theatre
115 MacDougal St
New York NY 10012
(212) 475-1237

Brazos Bookstore
2421 Bissonnet St
Houston TX 77005
(713) 523-0701

AMERICAN BOOKSTORE
DIRECTORY

Breakwater Books
81 Whitfield St
Guilford CT 06437
(203) 453-4141

Breck Books
100 North Main Street #201
Breckinridge CO 80424
(970) 771-3784

Brewster Book Store
2648 Main St
Brewster MA 02631
(508) 896-6543

Briars & Brambles Books
61 Route 296 and South St.
Windham NY 12496
(518) 750-8599

Brick & Mortar Books
7430 164th Ave NE Ste B105
Redmond WA 98052
(425) 869-0606

Bridge Street Books
2814 Pennsylvania Ave NW
Washington DC 20007
(202) 965-5200

Bridgeside Books

AMERICAN BOOKSTORE
DIRECTORY

29 Stowe St
Waterbury VT 05676
(802) 244-1441

Bright Ideas Books
1520 N Waterman Ave
San Bernardino CA 92404
(909) 888-3296

Bright Side Bookshop
18 N San Francisco St
Flagstaff AZ 86001
(928) 440-5041

Brilliant Books
118 E Front St
Traverse City MI 49684
(231) 946-2665

Broadside Bookshop
247 Main St
Northampton MA 01060
(413) 586-4235

Broadway Books
1714 NE Broadway St
Portland OR 97232
(503) 284-1726

Brock University Bookstore & Campus Store
500 Glenridge Ave

AMERICAN BOOKSTORE
DIRECTORY

St. Catharines ON L2S 3A1
(905) 688-5550

Bronco Bookstore
3801 W Temple Ave Bldg 66
Pomona CA 91768
(909) 869-3752

Bronx River Books
37 Spencer Place
Scarsdale NY 10583
(914) 420-6396

Brookline Booksmith
279 Harvard St
Brookline MA 02446
(617) 566-6660

Brooklyn Museum Shop
200 Eastern Pkwy
Brooklyn NY 11238
(718) 501-6341

Brooks Preik
The Cotton Exchange
Wilmington NC 28401
(910) 762-4444

Brown University Bookstore
244 Thayer St
Providence RI 02912

AMERICAN BOOKSTORE
DIRECTORY

(401) 863-3168

Browse Awhile Books
118 E Main St
Tipp City OH 45371
(937) 667-7200

Browseabout Books
133 Rehoboth Ave
Rehoboth Beach DE 19971
(302) 226-BOOK

Browser Books
2195 Fillmore St
San Francisco CA 94115
(415) 567-8027

Browsers Bookshop
107 Capitol Way N
Olympia WA 98501
(360) 5614929

Browsing Bison Books
515 Main St
Deer Lodge MT 59722
(406) 846-3288

Bryn Mawr College Book Shop
101 N Merion Ave
Bryn Mawr PA 19010
(610) 526-5321

AMERICAN BOOKSTORE
DIRECTORY

Bubba's Book Swap
331 E Sullivan St
Kingsport TN 37660
(423) 245-2847

Buffalo Books & Coffee
6 Division St E
Buffalo MN 55313
(763) 682-3147

Buffalo Street Books
215 N Cayuga St
Ithaca NY 14850
(607) 273-8246

Builders Booksource
1817 4th St
Berkeley CA 94710
(510) 845-6874

Bulk Bookstore
3330 NW Yeon Ave Suite 120
Portland OR 97210
(877) 650-5649

Bull Moose
17 Arbor St
Portland ME 04103
(207) 874-2123

AMERICAN BOOKSTORE
DIRECTORY

Bull Moose
Maine Square Mall
Bangor ME 04401
(207) 262-0410

Bull Moose
151 Maine St
Brunswick ME 04011
(207) 725-1289

Bull Moose
West St Shopping Plaza
Keene NH 03431
(603) 354-3591

Bull Moose
40 East Ave Ste 16
Lewiston ME 04240
(207) 784-6463

Bull Moose
219 Waterman Dr
South Portland ME 04106
(207) 347-2400

Bull Moose
Windham Shopping Center
North Windham ME 04062
(207) 893-1303

Bull Moose

151 Middle St
Portland ME 04101
(207) 780-6424

Bull Moose
82-86 Congress St
Portsmouth NH 03801
(603) 422-9525

Bull Moose
419 S Broadway
Salem NH 03079
(603) 898-6254

Bull Moose
Sanford ME 04073
(207) 324-5786

Bull Moose
456 Payne Rd
Scarborough ME 04074
(207) 885-9553

Bull Moose
80 Elm Plaza
Waterville ME 04901
(207) 861-5884

Bunch of Grapes Bookstore
23 Main St
Vineyard Haven MA 02568

AMERICAN BOOKSTORE
DIRECTORY

(508) 693-2291

Burgundy Books
1391 Boston Post Road
Old Saybrook CT 06475
(860) 391-9525

Burke's Book Store
936 S Cooper St
Memphis TN 38104
(901) 278-7484

Burlington by the Book
301 Jefferson St Ste 3
Burlington IA 52601
(319) 753-9981

Burrowing Owl Books
419 16th St
Canyon TX 79015
(806) 282-9888

Burry Bookstore
130 W Carolina Ave
Hartsville SC 29550
(843) 332-2511

Busboys and Poets
2004 Martin Luther King Jr. Avenue SE
Washington DC 20020
(202) 889-1374

AMERICAN BOOKSTORE
DIRECTORY

Busboys and Poets
625 Monroe St
Washington DC 20017
(202) 636-7230

Busboys and Poets
4251 S. Campbell Ave
Arlington VA 22206
(703) 379-9757

Busboys and Poets
235 Carroll St NW
Washington DC 20012
(202) 726-0856

Busboys and Poets
2021 14th St NW
Washington DC 20009
(202) 386-0804

Buteo Books
2731 Arrington Rd
Arrington VA 22922
(434) 263-8671

Butler University Bookstore
704 W. Hampton Dr
Indianapolis IN 46208
(317) 940-9228

AMERICAN BOOKSTORE
DIRECTORY

Butterfly 7
336 Malcolm X Blvd
Brooklyn NY 11233
(347) 240-7115

Buttonwood Books and Toys
747 Chief Justice Cushing Hwy Rte 3A
Cohasset MA 02025
(781) 383-2665

Buxton Books & Tours
160 King Street
Charleston SC 29401
(843) 834-6575

Buxton Village Books
47918 Highway 12
Buxton NC 27920
(252) 995-4240

Buy the Book
2894 S Huron Road
Kawkawlin MI 48631
(989) 684-3852

BW Bookstore
130 E Grand St
Berea OH 44017
(440) 826-2343

By Hand Ink

AMERICAN BOOKSTORE
DIRECTORY

71 Lighthouse Rd Ste 516
Hilton Head Island SC 29928
(843) 816-0860

By the Book Bookstore
702 Ayers St
Corpus Christi TX 78404
(361) 876-9990

Byrd's Books
178 Greenwood Ave
Bethel CT 06801
(203) 730-2973

BYU Bookstore
Brigham Young University
Provo UT 84602
(801) 422-3584

BYU-Idaho University Store
142 Manwaring Ctr
Rexburg ID 83460
(208) 496-3400

Cafe Con Libros
280 W 2nd St
Pomona CA 91766
(909) 469-1350

Cafe Con Libros
724 Prospect Pl

AMERICAN BOOKSTORE
DIRECTORY

Brooklyn NY 11216
(347) 460-2838

Calico Paw Books & Gifts
125 Boyd Ln
Henderson NC 27537
(919) 603-7260

Califon Book Shop
72 Main St
Califon NJ 07830
(908) 832-6686

CALTECH Bookstore
1-51 San Pasqual St
Pasadena CA 91125
(626) 395-6161

Camille Deboer
1938 Breton Rd SE
Grand Rapids MI 49506
(616) 942-9887

Canio's Books
290 Main St
Sag Harbor NY 11963
(631) 725-4926

Cannon Beach Book Company
130 N. Hemlock St. Suite 2
Cannon Beach OR 97110

AMERICAN BOOKSTORE
DIRECTORY

(503) 436-1301

Canterbury Book Store
908 Ludington St
Escanaba MI 49829
(906) 786-0751

Canvasback Books
9th Street Between Main St and Klamath Ave
Klamath Falls OR 97601
(541) 892-2497

Canyon Booksellers
736 N Main St
Spearfish SD 57783
(605) 717-2982

Capital Books
1011 K St
Sacramento CA 95814
(916) 492-6657

Caprichos Books
37 N Main St Suite 102
Bel Air MD 21014
(410) 929-6081

Card Carrying Books & Gifts
Market Street
Corning NY 14830
(607) 684-6114

AMERICAN BOOKSTORE
DIRECTORY

Carmichael's Bookstore
1295 Bardstown Rd
Louisville KY 40204
(502) 456-6950

Carmichael's Bookstore in Clifton
2720 Frankfort Ave
Louisville KY 40206
(502) 896-6950

Carmichael's Kids
1313 Bardstown Rd
Louisville KY 40204
(502) 709-4900

Carol's Paperbacks Plus
5947 Highland Rd
Waterford MI 48327
(248) 674-8179

Carroll & Carroll Booksellers
740 Main St
Stroudsburg PA 18360
(570) 420-1516

Carter's Books
217 S 13th Street
Griffin GA 30224
(770) 229-1188

AMERICAN BOOKSTORE
DIRECTORY

Casa Camino Real Book Store
314 South Tornillo Street
Las Cruces NM 88001
(575) 523-3988

Castlemere Books
575 1st St
Astoria OR 97103
(503) 325-4590

Cat and Mouse Games
1112 West Madison St
Chicago IL 60607
(312) 465-2178

Cavalier House Books
100 N Range Ave
Denham Springs LA 70726
(225) 664-2255

Cavener's Library & Office Supply
111 E Austin Blvd
Nevada MO 64772
(417) 667-2345

Caversham Booksellers
98 Harbord St
Toronto ON M5S 1G6
(416) 944-0962

AMERICAN BOOKSTORE
DIRECTORY

Cellar Door Books
5225 Canyon Crest Dr Ste 30A-B
Riverside CA 92507
(951) 787-7807

Central New Mexico Community College
Bookstore
725 University SE
Albuquerque NM 87106
(505) 243-0457

Centre College Bookstore
110 S 3rd St
Danville KY 40422
(859) 238-1516

Centuries & Sleuths Bookstore
7419 W. Madison Street
Forest Park IL 60130
(708) 771-7243

Cerritos College Bookstore
11190 Alondra Blvd
Norwalk CA 90650
(562) 860-2451

Chamblin Bookmine
4551 Roosevelt Blvd.
Jacksonville FL 32210
(904) 384-1685

AMERICAN BOOKSTORE
DIRECTORY

Chamblin's Uptown
215 N Laura St
Jacksonville FL 32202
(904) 384-1685

Changing Hands Bookstore
6428 S McClintock Dr
Tempe AZ 85283
(480) 730-1142

Changing Hands Bookstore
300 W Camelback Rd
Phoenix AZ 85013
(602) 274-0067

Chaparral Books
1975 SW 1st Ave. Suite L
Portland OR 97202
(503) 887-0823

Chapman University's Agora Gift shop
386 N. Center Street
Orange CA 92866
(714) 997-6718

Chapter 2
1180 McCall Rd
Cashiers NC 28717
(828) 743-5015

Chapter One Bookstore

AMERICAN BOOKSTORE
DIRECTORY

252 W Main St
Hamilton MT 59840
(406) 363-5220

Chapter One Bookstore
340 2nd Street E
Ketchum ID 83340
(208) 726-5425

Chapter Two Books
37 Spring Street
Williamstown MA 01267
(413) 884-6322

Chapter2Books
226 Locust St
Hudson WI 54016
(651) 239-4678

Chapters
31 N Main St
Miami OK 74354
(918) 540-0468

Chapters Books & Gifts
548 Seward St
Seward NE 68434
(402) 643-2282

Chapters Books and Coffee
701 E 1st St

AMERICAN BOOKSTORE
DIRECTORY

Newberg OR 97132
(503) 554-0206

Chapters Bookshop
101 E Grayson St
Galax VA 24333
(276) 236-9703

Chapters Bookstore
635 Haywood Road
Greenville SC 29607
(864) 281-1520

Chapters On Main
816 Main Street
Van Buren AR 72956
(479) 471-9315

Charis Books
184 S. Candler St
Decatur GA 30030
(404) 524-0304

Charleston Books
1916 Sam Rittenberg Blvd Apt 308
Charleston SC 29407
(843) 310-2712

Charlie's Corner
4102 24th St
San Francisco CA 94114

AMERICAN BOOKSTORE
DIRECTORY

(415) 641-1104

Charm City Books
782 Washington Blvd.
Baltimore MD 21230
(443) 682-9911

Chaucer's Books
3321 State St
Santa Barbara CA 93105
(805) 563-0010

Chautauqua Bookstore
67 Bestor Plaza
Chautauqua NY 14722
(716) 357-2151

Chelsea Antiques
2631 Durham Chapel Hill Blvd
Durham NC 27707
(919) 683-1865

Chequamegon Books
2 E Bayfield St
Washburn WI 54891
(715) 373-2899

Cherry Street Books
503 Broadway St
Alexandria MN 56308
(320) 763-9400

AMERICAN BOOKSTORE
DIRECTORY

Chevalier's Books
126 N Larchmont Blvd
Los Angeles CA 90004
(323) 465-1334

Chicago State University Bookstore
9501 S Martin L King Dr
Chicago IL 60628
(773) 995-2323

Chicago-Main Newsstand
860 Chicago Ave
Evanston IL 60202
(847) 425-8900

Chico State University Wildcat Store
101 Hazel Street
Chico CA 95928
(530) 898-5222

Children's Book Cellar
52 Main St
Waterville ME 04901
(207) 872-4543

Children's Book Garden
11809 Ocean Gtwy
Ocean City MD 21842
(410) 641-5800

AMERICAN BOOKSTORE
DIRECTORY

Children's Book World
10580 1/2 W Pico Blvd
Los Angeles CA 90064
(310) 559-2665

Children's Book World
17 Haverford Station Rd
Haverford PA 19041
(610) 642-6274

Chop Suey Books
2913 W Cary St
Richmond VA 23221
(804) 422-8066

Christopher's Books
1400 18th St
San Francisco CA 94107
(415) 255-8802

Church Street Coffee & Books
81 Church St
Birmingham AL 35213
(205) 870-1117

City Lights Books
261 Columbus Ave
San Francisco CA 94133
(415) 362-8193

City Lights Bookstore

AMERICAN BOOKSTORE
DIRECTORY

3 E Jackson St
Sylva NC 28779
(828) 586-9499

City Lit Books
2523 N Kedzie Blvd
Chicago IL 60647
(773) 235-2523

City News
4018 N Cicero Ave
Chicago IL 60641
(773) 545-7377

Civil Service Bookshop
34 Carmine St
New York NY 10014
(212) 226-9506

Claflin Books and Copies
1814 Claflin Rd
Manhattan KS 66502
(785) 776-3771

Clarkson University Bookstore
39 Market St
Potsdam NY 13676
(315) 265-9260

Classic Lines
5825 Forbes Ave

AMERICAN BOOKSTORE
DIRECTORY

Pittsburgh PA 15217
(412) 422-2220

Cleveland Museum of Natural History Store
University Circle
Cleveland OH 44106
(216) 231-4600 ext. 326

Cloud & Leaf Bookstore
148 Laneda Ave
Manzanita OR 97130
(503) 368-2665

Clues Unlimited
3154 E Fort Lowell Rd
Tucson AZ 85716
(520) 326-8533

Coastal Cottage Life
216 Haslin Street
Bellhaven NC 27810
(252) 943-4762

Coastside Books Inc.
432 A Main St
Half Moon Bay CA 94019
(650) 726-5889

Coffee Haven Books
76 Railroad St
Holliston MA 01746

AMERICAN BOOKSTORE
DIRECTORY

(508) 429-4106

CoffeeTree Books
159 E Main St
Morehead KY 40351
(606) 784-8364

Colgate Bookstore
3 Utica Street
Hamilton NY 13346
(315) 228-7480

Collected Works Bookstore & Coffeehouse
202 Galisteo St
Santa Fe NM 87501
(505) 988-4226

Collective Books
121 North Broadway
Rochester MN 55906
(507) 226-1021

Collector's Shangri-La
612 S Barrington Ave
Los Angeles CA 90049
(310) 766-4689

College of DuPage Bookstore
SRC Building
Glen Ellyn IL 60137
(630) 942-2361

AMERICAN BOOKSTORE
DIRECTORY

College of Saint Benedict Bookstore
37 South College Ave
St. Joseph MN 56374
(320) 363-3081

College of Southern Nevada Bookstore
6375 W Charleston Blvd
Las Vegas NV 89146
(702) 651-5606

Colorado State Univ. Bookstore
Colorado State University
Fort Collins CO 80523
(970) 491-1475

Columbia College Bookstore
624 S Michigan Ave
Chicago IL 60605
(312) 427-4860

Columbus State Community College Book
Store
283 Cleveland Ave
Columbus OH 43215
(614) 287-3695

Comickaze
5525 Clairemont Mesa Blvd
San Diego CA 92117
(858) 278-0371

AMERICAN BOOKSTORE
DIRECTORY

Common Language Bookstore
317 Braun Court
Ann Arbor MI 48104
(734) 663-0036

Commonplace Reader
49 S Main St
Yardley PA 19067
(215) 420-2620

Community Bookstore
143 7th Ave
Brooklyn NY 11215
(718) 783-3075

Compass Books at SFO (Terminal 2)
San Francisco International Airport
San Francisco CA 94128
(650) 821-9299

Compass Books at SFO (Terminal 3)
San Francisco International Airport
San Francisco CA 94128
(650) 821-2326

Compass Rose Books
3 Main St
Castine ME 04421
(207) 326-5034

AMERICAN BOOKSTORE
DIRECTORY

Completely Booked
201 Blue Spruce Way
Murrysville PA 15668
(724) 454-1862

Contemporary Jewish Museum
736 Mission St
San Francisco CA 94103
(415) 655-7888

Content Bookstore
314 Division St
Northfield MN 55057
(507) 222-9238

Copper Dog Books
272 Cabot St
Beverly MA 01915
(978) 969-3460

Copper News Bookstore
10 W Pajaro St
Ajo AZ 85321
(520) 387-7688

Copperfield's Books
Marin Country Mart
Larkspur CA 94939
(415) 870-9843

AMERICAN BOOKSTORE
DIRECTORY

Copperfield's Books
138 N Main St
Sebastopol CA 95472
(707) 823-2618

Copperfield's Books
8220 Louetta Rd Ste 106
Spring TX 77379
(832) 761-5559

Copperfield's Books
1330 Lincoln Ave
Calistoga CA 94515
(707) 942-1616

Copperfield's Books
106 Matheson St
Healdsburg CA 95448
(707) 433-9270

Copperfield's Books
775 Village Ct
Santa Rosa CA 95405
(707) 578-8938

Copperfield's Books
3740 Bel Aire Plaza
Napa CA 94558
(707) 252-8002

AMERICAN BOOKSTORE
DIRECTORY

Copperfield's Books
999 Grant Ave Ste S-105
Novato CA 94945
(415) 763-3052

Copperfield's Books
140 Kentucky St
Petaluma CA 94952
(707) 762-0563

Copperfield's Books
850 4th St
San Rafael CA 94901
(415) 524-2800

Copperfish Books
103 W Marion Ave
Punta Gorda FL 33950
(941) 205-2560

Corban University Bookstore
5000 Deer Park Drive SE
Salem OR 97317
(503) 375-7035

Corner Bookstore
43 N Jackson St
Winder GA 30680
(770) 867-5800

AMERICAN BOOKSTORE
DIRECTORY

Cornerstone Used Books
22 S Villa Ave
Villa Park IL 60181
(630) 254-2034

Country Bookshelf
28 W Main St
Bozeman MT 59715
(406) 587-0166

Country Sunshine
143 N Main St
Republic MO 65738
(417) 559-1197

Couth Buzzard Books Espresso Buono
8310 Greenwood Ave N
Seattle WA 98103
(206) 436-2960

Covered Treasures Bookstore
105 Second St
Monument CO 80132
(719) 481-2665

Cowboy Bookworm
4217 Arbor Gate St
Fort Worth TX 76133
(817) 238-3020

Crackerjacks Books

AMERICAN BOOKSTORE
DIRECTORY

7 S Washington St
Easton MD 21601
(410) 822-7716

Crazy Wisdom Bookstore
114 S Main St
Ann Arbor MI 48104
(734) 665-2757

Cream & Amber
1605 Main St
Hopkins MN 55343
(651) 983-4622

Creative Corner Books
245 River St
Hobart NY 13788
(240) 308-0563

Crimson and Mauve
4101 W Green Oaks Ste 305-125
Arlington TX 76016
(817) 405-2745

Crow Bookshop
14 Church St
Burlington VT 05401
(802) 862-0848

CSU at Dominguez Hills Bookstore
900 E Victoria St

AMERICAN BOOKSTORE
DIRECTORY

Carson CA 90746
(310) 243-3829

CSU at Northridge Bookstore
Cal State University
Northridge CA 91330
(818) 677-2932

CSU at Northridge Bookstore
18111 Nordhoff St
Northridge CA 91330
(818) 677-2932

CSU Sacramento Hornet Bookstore
Csu Sacramento
Sacramento CA 95819
(916) 278-6446

CSUEB Hayward Campus Pioneer Bookstore
25976 Carlos Bee Blvd
Hayward CA 94542
(510) 885-3507

Cultivator Bookstore
301 East Main St
Murfreesboro NC 27818
(252) 395-2327

Cupboard Maker Books
157 N Enola Rd
Enola PA 17025

AMERICAN BOOKSTORE
DIRECTORY

(717) 732-7288

Cuppa Pulp Writers' Space
817 Chestnut Ridge Rd
Chestnut Ridge NY 10977
(845) 671-8244

Cups and Books
2024 Bedford Avenue
Brookyln NY 11226
(718) 781-8398

Curious Book Shop
307 E Grand River Ave
East Lansing MI 48823
(517) 332-0112

Curious Iguana
12 N Market St
Frederick MD 21701
(301) 695-2500

Curmudgeon Books
7900 Ritchie Hwy
Glen Burnie MD 21061
(443) 410-0472

Daybreak Press Global Bookshop
720 Washington Avenue SE
Minneapolis MN 55414
(612) 584.3359

AMERICAN BOOKSTORE
DIRECTORY

DDR Books
7 S Maple
Watertown SD 57201
(605) 878-0418

Deals Stores
35 W State St
Media PA 19063
(610) 566-4643

Dee Gee's Gifts & Books
508 Evans St
Morehead City NC 28557
(252) 726-3314

Deep Vellum Books
3000 Commerce St
Dallas TX 75226
(972) 638-7741

Delaware Art Museum Store
2301 Kentmere Parkway
Wilmington DE 19806
(302) 351-8542

Delaware State University Bookstore
1200 N Dupont Hwy
Dover DE 19901
(302) 857-6225

AMERICAN BOOKSTORE
DIRECTORY

Delaware Technical Community College
Bookstore
Jason Technical Building
Georgetown DE 19947
(302) 259-6116

Des Moines Area Community College Bookstore
2006 S Ankeny Blvd
Ankeny IA 50023
(515) 964-6302

Destinations Booksellers
604 E Spring St
New Albany IN 47150
(812) 944-5116

Detecto Mysterioso
3037 Richmond St
Philadelphia PA 19134
(215) 923-0211

Devaney Doak & Garrett Booksellers
193 Broadway
Farmington ME 04938
(207) 778-3454

Diane's Books of Greenwich
8A Grigg Street
Greenwich CT 06830
(203) 869-1515

AMERICAN BOOKSTORE
DIRECTORY

DIESEL A Bookstore
225 26th St Ste 33
Santa Monica CA 90402
(510) 653-9965

DIESEL A Bookstore
12843 El Camino Real Suite 104
San Diego CA 92130
(858) 925-7078

Dimple Books
2499 Arden Way
Sacramento CA 95825
9169978848

Dimple Books
2433 Arden Way
Sacramento CA 95825
(916) 925-2600

Dimple Books
2500 16th St.
Sacramento CA 95818
(916) 441-2500

Dimple Books
7830 Macy Plaza Dr
Citrus Heights CA 95610
(916) 962-3600

Dimple Books

AMERICAN BOOKSTORE
DIRECTORY

313 E Bidwell St
Folsom CA 95630
(916) 983-2600

Dimple Books
1600 Broadway
Sacramento CA 95818
(916) 239-3750

Dimple Books
1129 Roseville Square
Roseville CA 95678
(916) 781-2800

Dog Ear Books
301 W Main St
Russellville AR 72801
(479) 219-5123

Dog Eared Books
900 Valencia St
San Francisco CA 94110
(415) 282-1901

Dog Eared Books
489 Castro St
San Francisco CA 94114
(415) 658-7920

Dog Ears Bookstore
688 Abbott Rd

AMERICAN BOOKSTORE
DIRECTORY

Buffalo NY 14220
(716) 823-2665

Dog Moon Books
544 E. Tri-County Blvd
Oliver Springs TN 37840
(865) 208-1618

Dolly's Bookstore
510 Main Street
Park City UT 84060
(435) 649-8062

Dotters Books
1602 Hogeboom Avenue
Eau Claire WI 54701
(414) 897-6258

Douglasville Books
6643 Church Street
Douglasville GA 30134
(770) 949-4363

Downbound Books
4139 Apple St.
Cincinnati OH 45223
(513) 541-1394

Downtown Book & News
67 N Lexington Ave
Asheville NC 28801

AMERICAN BOOKSTORE
DIRECTORY

(828) 253-8654

Downtown Book & Sound
213 Main Street
Salinas CA 93901
(831) 477-6700

Downtown Book & Toy
125 E High St
Jefferson City MO 65101
(573) 635-1185

Downtown Books
543 Yampa Ave
Craig CO 81625
(970) 824-5343

Downtown Books
105 Sir Walter Raleigh St
Manteo NC 27954
(252) 473-1056

Dragonfly Books
112 W Water St
Decorah IA 52101
(563) 382-4275

Dragonwings Bookstore
110 S Main St
Waupaca WI 54981
(715) 256-9186

AMERICAN BOOKSTORE
DIRECTORY

Drama Book Shop
250 W 40th St
New York NY 10018
(212) 944-0595

Driftless Books
518 Walnut St
Viroqua WI 54665
(608) 638-2665

Drury Lane Books
12 E Wisconsin St
Grand Marais MN 55604
(218) 387-3370

Duck River Books
12 Public Square
Columbia TN 38401
(931) 548-2665

Duck's Cottage
1240 Duck Rd
Duck NC 27949
(252) 261-5510

Dudad's Hallmark
236 5th Ave S
Clinton IA 52732
(309) 853-5029

AMERICAN BOOKSTORE
DIRECTORY

Dudley's Bookshop Cafe
135 NW Minnesota Ave
Bend OR 97701
(541) 749-2010

Duende District
1380 Monroe St NW Unit 422
Washington DC 20010
(505) 259-1484

Duke University Medical Center Bookstore
Duke Medical Center
Durham NC 27710
(919) 684-4373

Duke University Bookstore
Duke University Durham NC 27706
(919) 684-6793

Dunaway Books
3111 S Grand Blvd
St. Louis MO 63118
(314) 771-7150

Dundee Book Company
309 S 50th St
Omaha NE 68132
(402) 516-2141

Dutchess Community College Bookstore
53 Pendell Road

AMERICAN BOOKSTORE
DIRECTORY

Poughkeepsie NY 12601
(845) 431-8080

Eagle Eye Book Shop
2076 N Decatur Rd
Decatur GA 30033
(404) 486-0307

Eagle Harbor Book Company
157 Winslow Way East
Bainbridge Island WA 98110
2068425332

Earlham College Bookstore
Runyan Center
Richmond IN 47374
(765) 983-1310

Earthlight Bookstore
321 E Main St
Walla Walla WA 99362
(509) 525-4983

East Bay Booksellers
5433 College Ave
Oakland CA 94618
(510) 653-9965

East City Bookshop
645 Pennsylvania Ave SE Ste 100
Washington DC 20003

AMERICAN BOOKSTORE
DIRECTORY

(202) 669-7748

East End Books Ptown
389 Commercial St Unit 1
Provincetown MA 02657
(508) 413-9059

East Texas Baptist University Bookstore
Howard C Bennet Student Commons
Marshall TX 75670
(903) 923-2297

East West Bookshop of Seattle
6407 12th Ave NE
Seattle WA 98115
(206) 523-3726

Eastern Mennonite University Bookstore
1200 Park Rd
Harrisonburg VA 22802
(540) 432-4250

Eastern National
470 Maryland Dr
Fort Washington PA 19034
(215) 283-6900

Eastern National
3 Main St
Layton NJ 07851
(973) 948-0463

AMERICAN BOOKSTORE
DIRECTORY

Eastwind Books
2066 University Ave
Berkeley CA 94704
(510) 548-2350

Ebenezer Books
2 Lower Main W
Johnson VT 05655
(802) 635-7472

Eclectuals
5408 Whitewood Avenue
Lakewood CA 90712
(310) 283-9867

Ecology Center Bookstore
2530 San Pablo Ave
Berkeley CA 94702
(510) 548-3402

Ed's Editions
406 Meeting St
West Columbia SC 29169
(803) 791-8002

Edgartown Books
44 Main St.
Edgartown MA 02539
(508) 627-8463

AMERICAN BOOKSTORE
DIRECTORY

Edisto Island Bookstore
PO Box 420 547 Highway 174
Edisto Island SC 29438
(843) 869-1885

Edmonds Bookshop
111 5th Ave S
Edmonds WA 98020
(425) 775-2789

Edward McKay Used Books
1607 Battleground Ave
Greensboro NC 27408
(336) 274-4448

Edward McKay Used Books & More
115 Oakwood Dr
Winston-Salem NC 27103
(336) 724-6133

Eight Cousins
189 Main St
Falmouth MA 02540
(508) 548-5548

Eighth Day Bookstore
2838 E Douglas Ave
Wichita KS 67214
(316) 683-9446

El Taller Cafe & Bookstore

AMERICAN BOOKSTORE
DIRECTORY

275 Essex Street
Lawrence MA 01840
(978) 965-4145

Element of Fun
19 Rundel Park
Rochester NY 14607
(716) 930-2124

Eli's Bookstore
6 E. Washington St
Greencastle IN 46135
(765) 653-0618

Elk River Books
120 N Main St
Livingston MT 59047
(406) 224-5802

Ella Minnow Children's Bookstore
991 Kingston Rd
Toronto ON M4E1T3
(416) 698-5587

Ellen Plumb's City Bookstore
1122 Commercial St
Emporia KS 66801
(620) 208-2665

Elm Street Books
35 Elm St

AMERICAN BOOKSTORE
DIRECTORY

New Canaan CT 06840
(203) 966-4545

Elysian Fields
1273 S Tamiami Trl
Sarasota FL 34239
(941) 361-3006

Emerald Isle Books
8700 Emerald Dr
Emerald Isle NC 28594
(252) 354-5323

Emily Arrow Music
109 N Hobart Blvd
Los Angeles CA 90004
(310) 487-3552

Emily Books
150 Saint James Pl Apt 21
Brooklyn NY 11238
(415) 312-8770

Enchanted Chapters
10880 N 32nd St Suite 11
Phoenix AZ 85028
(480) 304-2652

Enchanted Passage
145 Armsby Rd
Sutton MA 01590

AMERICAN BOOKSTORE
DIRECTORY

(508) 841-5437

Epilogue Books
10 East Bridge St
Rockford MI 49341
(616) 884-0933

Epilogue Books
109 E Franklin St Suite 100
Chapel Hill NC 27517
(619) 410-2770

Ernest & Hadley Booksellers
1928 7th St
Tuscaloosa AL 35401
(205) 632-5331

Eureka Books
426 2nd St
Eureka CA 95501
(707) 444-9593

Every Thing Goes Book Cafe
208 Bay St
Staten Island NY 10301
(718) 447-8256

Everyone's Books
25 Elliot St
Brattleboro VT 05301
(802) 254-8160

AMERICAN BOOKSTORE
DIRECTORY

Excelsior Bay Books
36 Water St
Excelsior MN 55331
(952) 401-0932

Explore Booksellers & Bistro
221 E Main St
Aspen CO 81611
(970) 925-5336

Eye of Horus Metaphysical
910 W Lake St
Minneapolis MN 55408
(612) 872-1292

EyeSeeMe African American Children's
Bookstore
6951 Olive Blvd
University City MO 63130
(314) 349-1122

Fabled Bookshop & Cafe
217 South 4th St
Waco TX 76701
(817) 932-3094

Fables and Fairy Tales
38 N Main Street
Martinsville IN 46151
(765) 913-4100

AMERICAN BOOKSTORE
DIRECTORY

Fables Books
215 S. Main Street
Goshen IN 46526
(574) 534-1984

Face in a Book
4359 Town Center Blvd Ste 113
El Dorado Hills CA 95762
(916) 941-9401

Fact & Fiction
220 N Higgins Ave
Missoula MT 59802
(406) 721-2881

Fae Crate
117 Hillside Drive
Wetumpka AL 36092
(334) 350-0744

Fair Isle Books
1885 Detroit Harbor Rd
Washington Island WI 54246
(920) 847-2565

Fair Trade Books
320 Bush Street
Red Wing MN 55066
(651) 800-2030

AMERICAN BOOKSTORE
DIRECTORY

Fairfield University Bookstore
1499 Post Rd
Fairfield CT 06824
(203) 255-7756

Fairy Godmother
319 7th St SE
Washington DC 20003
(202) 547-5474

Faith and Life Bookstore
606 N Main St
Newton KS 67114
(316) 283-2210

Fallen Leaf Books
45 S Jefferson St
Nashville IN 47448
(812) 988-0202

Family Book Shop
1301 N Woodland Blvd
DeLand FL 32720
(386) 736-6501

Farley's Bookshop
44 S Main St
New Hope PA 18938
(215) 862-2452

Faulkner House Books

AMERICAN BOOKSTORE
DIRECTORY

624 Pirates Alley
New Orleans LA 70116
(504) 524-2940

Fenton's Open Book
105 W Shiawassee Ave
Fenton MI 48430
(810) 629-8000

Fenwick Street Used Books
41655A Fenwick Street
Leonardtown MD 20650
(301) 475-2859

Ferguson Books & More
1720 S Washington St
Grand Forks ND 58201
(701) 738-8025

Fiction Addiction
1175 Woods Crossing Rd Ste 5
Greenville SC 29607
(864) 675-0540

Field Museum Stores
1400 S Lake Shore Dr
Chicago IL 60605
(312) 665-7679

Fields Book Store
3060 El Cerrito Plaza #360

AMERICAN BOOKSTORE
DIRECTORY

El Cerrito CA 94530
(415) 673-2027

Fieldstone Book Company
637 Wyckoff Ave Ste 355
Wyckoff NJ 07481
(201) 891-8444

Fine Print Booksellers
28 Dock Square Unit 6
Kennebunkport ME 04046
(207) 752-0030

Finley's Fiction
9 Washington Street
Shelter Island Heights NY 11963
(203) 650-7616

Firefly Bookstore
271 W Main St
Kutztown PA 19530
(484) 648-2712

Fireside Book Shop
29 N Franklin St
Chagrin Falls OH 44022
(440) 247-4050

Fireside Books
720 S Alaska St
Palmer AK 99645

(907) 745-2665

Firestorm Books & Coffee
610 Haywood Rd
Asheville NC 28806
(828) 255-8115

Flagler College Bookstore
50 Sevilla St
Saint Augustine FL 32084
(904) 825-4681

Flashlight Books
1537 North Main Street
Walnut Creek CA 94596
(617) 953-2791

Fleur Fine Books
1720 Magnolia Ave Ste 104
Port Neches TX 77651
(409) 344-0876

Flights of Fantasy Books
381 Sand Creek Rd
Albany NY 12205
(518) 435-9337

Flights of Imagination
4759 Winterberry Ct
Williamsburg VA 23188
(757) 221-8212

AMERICAN BOOKSTORE
DIRECTORY

Flintridge Bookstore & Coffee House
101 Foothill Blvd
La Canada CA 91011
(818) 790-0717

Florida Atlantic University Bookstore
777 Glades Road
Boca Raton FL 33431
(561) 297-3720

Florida Gulf Coast University Bookstore
11090 FGCU BLVD N
Fort Myers FL 33965
(239) 590-1150

Florida State University Bookstore
104 N Woodward Ave.
Tallahassee FL 32304
(850) 644-2072

Flyleaf Books
752 Martin Luther King Jr Blvd
Chapel Hill NC 27514
(919) 942-7373

Foggy Pine Books
471 W King St
Boone NC 28607
(828) 386-1219

AMERICAN BOOKSTORE
DIRECTORY

Folger Shakespeare Library Shop
201 E Capitol St SE
Washington DC 20003
(202) 675-0312

Folio Books
3957 24th St
San Francisco CA 94114
(415) 821-3477

Foothill College Book Store
12345 S El Monte Rd Los Altos Hills CA 94022
(650) 949-7308

For Keeps Books
171 Auburn Avenue H1
Atlanta GA 30303
(404) 662-3319

Forever Books
312 State St St.
Joseph MI 49085
(269) 982-1110

Fort Lewis College Bookstore
1000 Rim Drive
Durango CO 81301
(970) 247-7415

Fort Valley State University Bookstore
1005 State University Dr

Fort Valley GA 31030
(478) 825-6623

Four Seasons Books
116 W German St Shepherdstown WV 25443
(304) 876-3486

Four-Eyed Frog Books
39138 Ocean Dr Gualala CA 95445
(707) 884-1333

Fox's Book Adventures
Logan OH 43138
(740) 385-0400

FoxTale Book Shoppe
105 E Main St Ste 138
Woodstock GA 30188
(770) 516-9989

Francie & Finch Bookshop
130 S. 13th St Suite 100
Lincoln NE 68508
(402) 781-0459

Frederick Community College
7932 Opossumtown Pike
Frederick MD 21702
(310) 846-2544

Frenchmen Art & Books

AMERICAN BOOKSTORE
DIRECTORY

600 Frenchmen Street
New Orleans LA 70116
(504) 301-7787

Fresno Pacific University Bookshop
1717 S Chestnut Ave
Fresno CA 93702
(559) 453-2078

Friends of Art Bookshop
1201 E 7th St
Bloomington IN 47405
(812) 855-1333

From My Shelf Books & Gifts
7 East Ave Suite 101
Wellsboro PA 16901
(570) 724-5793

Front Street Books
121 E Holland Ave
Alpine TX 79830
(432) 837-3360

Frugal Frigate a Children's Bookstore
9 N 6th St
Redlands CA 92373
(909) 793-0470

Frugal Muse Books
7511 Lemont Rd

AMERICAN BOOKSTORE
DIRECTORY

Darien IL 60561
(630) 427-1140

Full Circle Bookstore
1900 NW Expressway Suite 135
Oklahoma City OK 73118
(405) 842-2900

G.J. Ford Bookshop
600 Sea Island Rd
Saint Simons Island GA 31522
(912) 634-6168

Galapagos Books
22A Main St
Hastings-on-Hudson NY 10706
(914) 478-2501

Galiano Island Books
A201 20159 88th Avenue
Langley BC V1M 0A4
(250) 539-3340

Gallery Bookshop
319 Kasten St
Mendocino CA 95460
(707) 937-2665

Gamble House Bookstore
4 Westmoreland Pl
Pasadena CA 91103

(626) 793-3334

Gansevoort House Books
410 Canal Pl
Little Falls NY 13365
(315) 823-3969

Garcia Street Books
376 Garcia St
Santa Fe NM 87501
(505) 986-0151

Garcia Street Books
376 Garcia St
Santa Fe NM 87501
(505) 986-0151

Garden District Book Shop
2727 Prytania St
New Orleans LA 70130
(504) 895-2266

Gardner's Used Books and Music
4419 S Mingo Rd
Tulsa OK 74146
(918) 627-7323

Gathering Volumes
196 E. South Boundary
Perrysburg OH 43551
(567) 336-6188

AMERICAN BOOKSTORE
DIRECTORY

Gatsby Books
5535 E Spring St
Long Beach CA 90808
(562) 208-5862

Gene's Books
2365 Periwinkle Way
Sanibel FL 33957
(941) 202958

George Washington University Bookstore
800 21st Street NW
Washington DC 20052
(202) 676-6870

Georgetown University Bookstore (B&N Store)
Leavey Center
Washington DC 20007
(202) 687-7482

Georgia Southern University Armstrong
Bookstore
11935 Abercorn Street
Savannah GA 31419
(912) 344-2603

Georgia State University Bookstore
66 Courtland St
Atlanta GA 30303
(404) 413-9700

AMERICAN BOOKSTORE
DIRECTORY

Get Lit Bookshop
1502 East Fry Blvd
Sierra Vista AZ 85635
(520) 678-9310

Gettysburg College Bookstore
College Union Building
Gettysburg PA 17325
(717) 337-6367

Gibson's Bookstore
45 South Main Street
Concord NH 03301
(603) 224-0562

Givens Books
2236 Lakeside Dr
Lynchburg VA 24501
(434) 385-5027

Gladewater Books
2025 Ashley Dr
Gladewater TX 75647
(903) 720-3098

Globus Books
332 Balboa St.
San Francisco CA 94118
(415) 668-4723

AMERICAN BOOKSTORE
DIRECTORY

Gloria Deo
5601 S 56th St Ste 15
Lincoln NE 68516
(402) 420-1830

Gloria Deo
13065 W Center Rd
Omaha NE 68144
(402) 898-4633

Glow Worm Used Books
310 Main St
Spring TX 77373
(281) 253-0782

Godfather's Books
1108 Commercial St
Astoria OR 97103
(503) 325-8143

GoGo Books
40 East Main Street #185
Newark DE 19711
(302) 388-7167

Golden Fig Books
2706 Durham Chapel Hill Blvd
Durham NC 27707
(704) 641-6040

AMERICAN BOOKSTORE
DIRECTORY

Gone Fishing Books
113 Main St Floor 2
Lenoir NC 28645
(919) 923-8251

Gonzaga University Bookstore
801 E Desmet Ave
Spokane WA 99202
(509) 313-6390

Gordon College Bookstore
255 Grapevine Rd
Wenham MA 01984
(978) 867-4085

Gottwals Books
1806 Russell Pkwy Ste 1400
Warner Robins GA 31088
(478) 225-1044

Gottwals Books
311 GA HWY 49 N Ste 190
Byron GA 31008
(478) 956-0333

Gottwals Books
2834 Riverside Dr
Macon GA 31204
(478) 477-9200

AMERICAN BOOKSTORE
DIRECTORY

Gottwals Books
909 Carroll St
Perry GA 31069
(478) 988-4842

Gramercy Books
2424 E Main St Ste 100
Bexley OH 43209
(614) 867 5515

Grand Valley Books
350 Main St
Grand Junction CO 81501
(970) 424-5437

Grandpa's Barn
385 S Fourth St
Copper Harbor MI 49918
(906) 289-4704

Grass Roots Books & Music
227 SW 2nd St
Corvallis OR 97333
(541) 754-7668

Grassroots Books
660 E Grove St
Reno NV 89502
(775) 828-2665

Greedy Reads

AMERICAN BOOKSTORE
DIRECTORY

1744 Aliceanna Street
Baltimore MD 21231
(410) 276-6222

Green Apple Books
506 Clement St
San Francisco CA 94118
(415) 387-2272

Green Apple Books
1231 9th Ave
San Francisco CA 94122
(415) 742-5833

Green Bean Books
1600 NE Alberta St
Portland OR 97211
(503) 954-2354

Green Mountain Books
1055 Broad St
Lyndonville VT 05851
(802) 626-5051

Greenlight Bookstore
686 Fulton St
Brooklyn NY 11217
(718) 246-0200

Griffin Bay Bookstore
155 Spring St

AMERICAN BOOKSTORE
DIRECTORY

Friday Harbor WA 98250
(360) 378-5511

Guidon Books
7109 E 2nd St
Scottsdale AZ 85251
(480) 945-8811

Gwen's Book Mart
518 SE Riverside Dr
Evansville IN 47713
(812) 401-1050

Half Moon Books
35 N Front St
Kingston NY 12401
(845) 331-5439

Half Price Books
4685 Cypress Creek Parkway
Houston TX 77069
(281) 583-9992

Hardin-Simmons University Bookstore
2200 Hickory Street
Abilene TX 79698
(325) 677-2332

Harpers Ferry Historical Association Bookstore
723 Shenandoah St
Harpers Ferry WV 25425

AMERICAN BOOKSTORE
DIRECTORY

(304) 535-6881

Hartfield Book Company
110 W Washington St
Monticello IL 61856
(217) 631-1900

Harvard Book Store
1256 Massachusetts Ave
Cambridge MA 02138
(617) 661-1515

Harvey's Tales
216 James St
Geneva IL 60134
(630) 232-2991

Haverford College Bookstore
370 Lancaster Ave
Haverford PA 19041
(610) 896-1177

HearthFire Books and Treats
1254 Bergen Pkwy
Evergreen CO 80439
(303) 670-4549

Hearthside Books & Toys
254 Front St
Juneau AK 99801
(907) 586-1726

Hearthside Books & Toys
8745 Glacier Hwy
Juneau AK 99801
(907) 789-2750

Hedgie's Books
414 Main St Bedford IA 50833
(712) 523-2371

Henderson Books
116 Grand Ave
Bellingham WA 98225
(360) 734-6855

Hennessey & Ingalls
300 S Santa Fe Ave Ste M
Los Angeles CA 90013
(213) 437-2130

Here's A Book Store
1964 Coney Island Ave
Brooklyn NY 11223
(718) 645-6675

Herringbone Books
422 SW 6th St
Redmond OR 97756
(541) 526-1491

Hicklebee's

AMERICAN BOOKSTORE
DIRECTORY

1378 Lincoln Ave
San Jose CA 95125
(408) 292-8880

Hickory Stick Bookshop
2 Green Hill Rd
Washington Depot CT 06793
(860) 868-0525

Hideaway Books
2240 Gateway Oaks Drive Apt 120
Sacramento CA 95833
(831) 275-5182

High Five Books
29 N Maple St
Florence MA 01062
(515) 205-9855

Highland Books
36 W Main St
Brevard NC 28712
(828) 884-2424

Hilbert College Bookstore
5200 S Park Ave
Hamburg NY 14075
(716) 648-3604

Hills & Hamlets Bookshop
10625 Serenbe Ln

AMERICAN BOOKSTORE
DIRECTORY

Chattahoochee GA 30268
(678) 977-5517

Hipocampo Children's Books
638 South Ave
Rochester NY 14609
(585) 461-0161

Hiram Books
50 Darby's Crossing
Hiram GA 30141
(770) 480-9190

Hiram College Bookstore
11730 State Route 700
Hiram OH 44234
(330) 569-5209

Historic Deerfield Museum Store
84B Old Main St
Deerfield MA 01342
(413) 775-7171

Hobart International Bookport
615 Main St
Hobart NY 13788
(607) 538-3010

Hockessin Book Shelf
7179 Lancaster Pike
Hockessin DE 19707

AMERICAN BOOKSTORE
DIRECTORY

(302) 235-7665

Holy Trinity Monastery Bookstore
1407 Robinson Rd
Jordanville NY 13361
(315) 858-3817

Honest Dog Books
40 South Second Street
Bayfield WI 54814
(715) 779-5223

Hooked On Books
81909 Overseas Hwy
Islamorada FL 33036
(305) 517-2602

Hooray for Books
1555 King St
Alexandria VA 22314
(703) 548-4092

Hope Geneva Bookstore
Hope College
Holland MI 49423
(616) 395-7833

Hopkins Book Shop
5171 Shelburne Rd
Shelburne VT 05401
(802) 658-6223

AMERICAN BOOKSTORE
DIRECTORY

Horizon Books
243 East Front Street
Traverse City MI 49684
(231) 946-7290

Horizon Books
115 South Mitchell
Cadillac MI 49601
(231) 775-9979

Horton's Books & Gifts
410 Adamson Sq
Carrollton GA 30117
(770) 832-8021

House of Books and Games
1073 Palisado Ave
Windsor CT 06095
(860) 219-0393

Housing Works Bookstore
126 Crosby St
New York NY 10012
(212) 334-3324

Hub City Bookshop
186 W Main St
Spartanburg SC 29306
(864) 577-9349

AMERICAN BOOKSTORE
DIRECTORY

Huckleberry Books
16 9th Ave S
Cranbrook BC V1C 2L8
(250) 426-3415

Hudson Booksellers
1521 Johnson Ferry Rd Ste 250
Marietta GA 30062
(678) 560-5967

Hudson Booksellers BWI (625)
Baltimore Washington Int'l - Hudson Group
Baltimore MD 21240
(410) 859-5500

Hudson Booksellers CITI (1052)
CitiGroup - Hudson News
Chicago IL 60661
(312) 441-0043

Hudson Booksellers CLE C360 (736)
Cleveland Hopkins Int'l - Hudson News
Cleveland OH 44135
(216) 265-8487

Hudson Booksellers CLE MT 120 (726)
Cleveland Hopkins Int'l - Hudson News
Cleveland OH 44135
(216) 265-8487

Hudson Booksellers DEN (1100)

AMERICAN BOOKSTORE
DIRECTORY

Denver Int'l - Hudson News
Denver CO 80249
(303) 342-6802

Hudson Booksellers EWR (940)
Newark Liberty Int'l - Hudson News
Elizabeth NJ 07201
(973) 622-3143

Hudson Booksellers EWR A11 (778)
Newark Liberty Int'l - Hudson News
Elizabeth NJ 07114
(973) 622-3143

Hudson Booksellers EWR C1 (396)
Newark Liberty Int'l - Hudson News
Elizabeth NJ 07114
(973) 622-3143

Hudson Booksellers EWR C118A (916)
Newark Liberty Int'l - Hudson News
Elizabeth NJ 07201
(973) 622-3143

Hudson Booksellers LGA (1047)
LaGuardia Airport - Hudson News
Flushing NY 11371
(718) 424-6500

Hudson Booksellers LGA (357)
LaGuardia Airport - Hudson News

AMERICAN BOOKSTORE
DIRECTORY

Flushing NY 11371
(718) 424-6500

Hudson Booksellers MDW (1783)
Midway Distribution Ctr - Hudson News Chicago
IL 60638
(773) 735-0505

Hudson Booksellers MSY (1193)
New Orleans Int'l - Hudson News
Kenner LA 70062
(504) 443-0388

Hudson Booksellers OMA (443)
Omaha Int'l - Hudson News
Omaha NE 68110
(402) 341-9760

Hudson Booksellers PENN (224)
Penn Station - Hudson News
New York NY 10001
(212) 971-6800

Hudson Booksellers PIT (422)
Pittsburgh Int'l - Hudson/WDFG
Pittsburgh PA 15231
(412) 472-3175

Hudson Booksellers PIT (481)
Pittsburgh Int'l - Hudson/WDFG

AMERICAN BOOKSTORE
DIRECTORY

Pittsburgh PA 15231
(412) 472-3175

Hudson Booksellers PIT (482)
Pittsburgh Int'l - Hudson/WDFG
Pittsburgh PA 15231
(412) 472-3175

Hudson Booksellers SEA CT-10 (1110)
SEATAC - Hudson News
Seatac WA 98148
(206) 244-2984

Hudson Booksellers SEA/TAC (571)
SEATAC - Hudson News
Seatac WA 98148
(206) 244-2984

Hudson Booksellers SJC (1491)
Mineta San Jose Int'l - Hudson News
San Jose CA 95131
(408) 441-2635

Hudson Booksellers/Vroman's LAX (985)
Los Angeles Int'l - Hudson News
Carson CA 90746
(310) 338-2053

Hudson County Community College Bookstore
162 Sip Avenue

AMERICAN BOOKSTORE
DIRECTORY

Jersey City NJ 07306
(201) 360-4390

Hudson News ABQ KIOSK A-5 (315)
Albuquerque Int'l - Hudson News
Albuquerque NM 87119
(505) 764-3017

Hue-Man Bookstore
PO Box 5541
New York NY 10027
(646) 480-2268

Humboldt State University Bookstore
1 E Laurel Dr
Arcata CA 95521
(707) 826-3958

Huntley Bookstore of Claremont College
175 E 8th St
Claremont CA 91711
(909) 607-1502

Husky Central Store
1319 4th Avenue
Seattle WA 98101
(206) 685.9920

I AM Books Inc.
189 North St
Boston MA 02113

AMERICAN BOOKSTORE
DIRECTORY

(857) 263-7665

I Know You Like A Book
4707 N Prospect Rd
Peoria Heights IL 61616
(309) 685-2665

I Love Books
380 Delaware Ave
Delmar NY 12054
(518) 478-0715

I Love Books Bookstore
2101 Fort Henry Dr
Kingsport TN 37664
(423) 378-5859

Iconoclast Books & Gifts
111 N First St
Hailey ID 83333
(208) 726-1564

Ideas Bookstore
2234 Kimberton Rd
Phoenixville PA 19460
(610) 933-3742

Idlewild Books
170 7th Ave S
New York NY 10014
(212) 414-8888

AMERICAN BOOKSTORE
DIRECTORY

Idlewild Brooklyn
249 Warren St
Brooklyn NY 11201
(718) 403-9600

Iliad Bookshop
5400 Cahuenga Blvd
North Hollywood CA 91601
(818) 509-2665

Illini Union Bookstore
809 S Wright St
Champaign IL 61820
(217) 333-2050

Indiana-Purdue University Bookstore
2101 E Coliseum BLVD
Fort Wayne IN 46805
(260) 481-0300

Inisfree Bookshop
312 Daniel Webster Hwy
Meredith NH 03253
(603) 279-3905

Inquiring Minds Bookstore
6 Church St
New Paltz NY 12561
(845) 255-8300

Inquiring Minds Bookstore

AMERICAN BOOKSTORE
DIRECTORY

65 Partition Street
Saugerties NY 12477
(845) 246-5775

Island Books
3014 78th Ave SE
Mercer Island WA 98040
(206) 232-6920

Island Bookstore
1130 Corolla Village Rd
Corolla NC 27927
(252) 453-2292

Island Bookstore
1177 Duck Road
Kitty Hawk NC 27949
(252) 453-2292

Jabberwocky Bookshop & Cafe
50 Water St
Newburyport MA 01950
(978) 465-9359

Jackson Hole Book Trader
970 W Broadway Ste A
Jackson WY 83002
(307) 734-6001

Jackson State University Bookstore
1400 JR Lynch St

AMERICAN BOOKSTORE
DIRECTORY

Jackson MS 39217
(601) 979-2021

Jake's Place Books
142 Harrison St
Oak Park IL 60304
(312) 470-3135

James Madison University Bookstore
211 Blue Stone Dr
Harrisonburg VA 22807
(540) 568-6296

Kingsborough Community College Bookstore
2001 Oriental Blvd RM U-101
Brooklyn NY 11235
(718) 332-6900

Kinokuniya Bookstore
6929 Airport Blvd #121
Austin TX 78752
(512) 291-2026

Kinokuniya Bookstores
10500 SW Beaverton Hillsdale Hwy
Beaverton OR 97005
(503) 641-6240

Kinokuniya Bookstores
2540 Old Denton Road Suite 114
Carrollton TX 75006

AMERICAN BOOKSTORE
DIRECTORY

(214) 731.6800

Kinokuniya Bookstores
100 E. Algonquin Road
Arlington Heights IL 60005
(847) 427-2665

Kinokuniya Bookstores
123 Astronaut E. S. Onizuka Street
Los Angeles CA 90012
(213) 687-4480

Kinokuniya Bookstores
595 River Road
Edgewater NJ 07020
(201) 496-6910

Kinokuniya Bookstores
1073 Ave of the Americas
New York NY 10018
(212) 869-1700

Kinokuniya Bookstores
100 Legacy Drive
Plano TX 75023
(972) 517-0226

Kinokuniya Bookstores
1581 Webster St
San Francisco CA 94115
(415) 567-7625

AMERICAN BOOKSTORE
DIRECTORY

Kinokuniya Bookstores
685 Saratoga Ave
San Jose CA 95129
(408) 252-1300

Kinokuniya Bookstores
3760 South Centinela Avenue
Los Angeles CA 90066
(310) 482-3382

Kinokuniya Bookstores
525 S Weller St
Seattle WA 98104
(206) 587-2477

Lowry's Books
118 W Chicago Rd
Sturgis MI 49091
(269) 651-6817

Lowry's Books
22 N Main
Three Rivers MI 49093
(269) 273-7323

Loyalty Bookstore
827 Upshur St NW
Washington DC 20011
(202) 726-0380

AMERICAN BOOKSTORE
DIRECTORY

Lucy's Books
348 12th St
Astoria OR 97103
(503) 325-4210

Main Street Books
426 Main St
Lafayette IN 47901
(765) 464-6794

Main Street Books
46 Main St
Orleans MA 02653
(508) 255-3343

Main Street Books
2 E. Main St.
Frostburg MD 21532
(301) 689-5605

Main Street Books
307 S Main St
St. Charles MO 63301
(636) 949-0105

Main Street Books
205 Main Street
Hattiesburg MS 39407
(601) 584-6960

Main Street Books

AMERICAN BOOKSTORE
DIRECTORY

126 S Main St
Davidson NC 28036
(704) 892-6841

Main Street Books
8 Main St S
Minot ND 58701
(701) 839-4050

Main Street Books
104 N Main St
Mansfield OH 44902
707-963-1338

Main Street Books
110 E Main St
Monroe WA 98272
(360) 794-2976

Main Street Reads
115 South Main Street
Summerville SC 29483
(843) 875-5171

M and M Bookstore
212 Edgewood Rd NW
Cedar Rapids IA 52405
(319) 396-8420

M. Judson Booksellers
130 S Main St

AMERICAN BOOKSTORE
DIRECTORY

Greenville SC 29601
(864) 603-2412

Politics and Prose
70 District Square SW
Washington DC 20024
(202) 488-3867

Politics and Prose
1270 5th Street NE
Washington DC 20002
(202) 544-4565

Politics and Prose Bookstore
5015 Connecticut Ave NW
Washington DC 20008
(202) 364-1919

Powell's Books
7 NW 9th Ave
Portland OR 97209
(503) 228-0540

Powell's Books
3415 SW Cedar Hills Blvd
Beaverton OR 97005
(503) 228-4651

Powell's Books
7000 NE Airport Way
Portland OR 97218

AMERICAN BOOKSTORE
DIRECTORY

(503) 228-4651

Powell's Books
3747 SE Hawthorne Blvd
Portland OR 97214
(503) 235-3802

Powell's Books
3723 SE Hawthorne Blvd
Portland OR 97214
(503) 238-1668

Powell's City of Books
1005 W Burnside St
Portland OR 97209
(503) 228-4651

Queen Anne Book Company
1811 Queen Anne Ave N
Seattle WA 98109
(206) 284-2427

R.J. Julia Booksellers
768 Boston Post Rd
Madison CT 06443
(203) 245-3959

The Book Mark
800 W College Ave
St. Peter MN 56082
(507) 933-7587

AMERICAN BOOKSTORE
DIRECTORY

The Book Nerd
70 Maple Ave
Barrington RI 02806
(401) 337-5228

The Book Nook
8744 Ferry St
Montague MI 49437
(231) 894-5333

The Book Nook
6944 N University St
Peoria IL 61614
(309) 693-3612

The Book Nook
42 S Monroe St
Monroe MI 48161
(734) 241-2665

The Book Nook
181 N Grant St.
Canby OR 97013
(503) 9199895

The Book Nook
130 E Philadelphia Ave
Boyertown PA 19512
(610) 473-0925

AMERICAN BOOKSTORE
DIRECTORY

The Book Nook
130 E Philadelphia Ave
Boyertown PA 19512
(610) 473-0925

The Book Nook
7 Broadway
Saranac Lake NY 12983
(631) 599-9511

The Book Nook
108 S Douglas St
Brenham TX 77833
(979) 836-7323

The Book Nook
136 Main St
Ludlow VT 05149
(802) 228-3238

The Book Nook
641 N Cummings Ln
Washington IL 67571
(309) 508-7323

The Book Rack
878 Middle Rd
Bettendorf IA 52722
(563) 355-2310

The Book Rack

AMERICAN BOOKSTORE
DIRECTORY

4061 E Wesley Ave
Denver CO 80222
(303) 756-9891

The Book Rack
13 Medford St
Arlington MA 02474
(781) 646-2665

The Book Rack
50 S Plaza Way
Cape Girardeau MO 63703
(573) 334-2711

The Book Rack
8315 Beechmont Ave Ste 23
Cincinnati OH 45255
(513) 474-1337

The Booksmith
1644 Haight St
San Francisco CA 94117
(415) 863-8688

The Last Bookstore
453 S Spring St
Los Angeles CA 90013
(213) 488-0599

UC Davis Bookstore
1 Shields Ave

AMERICAN BOOKSTORE
DIRECTORY

Davis CA 95616
(530) 752-9072

UC San Diego Bookstore
9500 Gilman Dr
La Jolla CA 92093
(858) 534-7323

UCLA Bookzone
308 Westwood Plz
Los Angeles CA 90095
(310) 206-0764

UCSB Bookstore
University Of California
Santa Barbara CA 93106
(805) 893-2330

UMass Boston Bookstore
100 Morrissey Blvd
Dorchester MA 02125
(617) 287-5090

UMass Lowell Campus Bookstore
220 Pawtucket St
Lowell MA 01854
978-934-2623

Vermont Book Shop
38 Main St
Middlebury VT 05753

AMERICAN BOOKSTORE
DIRECTORY

(802) 388-2061

Victor Lundeen Company
126 W Lincoln Ave
Fergus Falls MN 56537
(800) 346-4870

Viewpoint Books
548 Washington St
Columbus IN 47201
(812) 376-0778

Village Books
1810A Paris Rd
Columbia MO 65201
(573) 449-8637

Village Books
344 N State St
Ukiah CA 95482
(707) 468-5355

Village Books
1200 11th St
Bellingham WA 98225
(360) 671-2626

Village Books
430 Front St
Lynden WA 98264
(360) 671-2626

AMERICAN BOOKSTORE
DIRECTORY

Villanova University Bookstore
Kennedy Hall
Villanova PA 19085
(610) 519-416

Vintage Books
6613 E Mill Plain Blvd
Vancouver WA 98661
(360) 694-9519

Vroman's Bookstore
695 E Colorado Blvd
Pasadena CA 91101
(626) 449-5320

Vroman's Hastings Ranch
3729 E Foothill Blvd
Pasadena CA 91107
(626) 449-5320

Wake Forest University Bookstore
Taylor Bookstore
Winston-Salem NC 27106
(336) 758-5145

Wakefield Books
160 Old Tower Hill Rd
Wakefield RI 02879
(401) 792-0000

AMERICAN BOOKSTORE
DIRECTORY

Walden Pond Books
3316 Grand Ave
Oakland CA 94610
(510) 832-4438

Watchung Booksellers
54 Fairfield St
Montclair NJ 07042
(973) 744-7177

Water Street Bookstore
125 Water Street
Exeter NH 03833
(603) 778-9731

Watermark Books & Cafe
4701 E Douglas Ave
Wichita KS 67218
(316) 682-1181

Waucoma Bookstore
212 Oak St
Hood River OR 97031
(541) 386-5353

Weller Book Works
607 Trolley Square
Salt Lake City UT 84102
(801) 328-2586

Wellesley Books

AMERICAN BOOKSTORE
DIRECTORY

82 Central St
Wellesley MA 02482
(781) 431-1160

Wellington Square Bookshop
549 Wellington Sq
Exton PA 19341
(610) 458-1144

Wendel's Bookstore
103-9233 Glover Road
Fort Langley BC V1M 2S5
(604) 513-2238

Western Michigan University Bookstore
1922 W Michigan Ave
Kalamazoo MI 49008
(269) 387-3930

Westwinds Bookshop
35 Depot St
Duxbury MA 02331
(781) 934-2128

WordsWorth Books
5920 R Street,
Little Rock, AR, 72207
(501) 663-9198

AMERICAN BOOKSTORE DIRECTORY

Why Bookstores Are Remaining Profitable

Many bookstore customers have expressed that their patronage of bookstores is related to the bookstore's level of interaction with the community. Community interaction involves book signings authors as guest speakers talking about their newest book attentive customer service staff that recommend books and creating an atmosphere where patrons can comfortably spend many hours reading. Bookstores are in many ways treated as modern libraries and patrons spend their time reading many books before purchasing. The patronage of the customer includes purchasing books purchasing point of sale items including bookmarks buying coffee and referring friends to visit the store. Even as major franchises are closing bookstores small bookstores have been thriving because they have less overhead and their attention to customers is greater thus their profit per square meter of retail floor space is higher making them profitable. The "stack 'em high sell 'em cheap" philosophy has worked for other products such as food items but book sales depend on close interaction between the customer and the bookstore employee.

AMERICAN BOOKSTORE DIRECTORY

MIKAZUKI PUBLISHING HOUSE™
(U.S.P.T.O. Serial Number 85705702)

1) 25 Principles of Martial Arts
2) 25 Principles of Strategy
3) American Antifa
4) American Bookstore Directory
5) Arctic Black Gold
6) Art of War
7) Back to Gold
8) Basketball Team Play Design Book
9) Beginner's Magicians Manual
10) Boxing Coloring Book
11) California's Next Century 2.0
12) Camping Survival Handbook
12) Captain Bligh's Voyage
13) Coming to America Handbook
14) Customer Sales Organizer
15) DIY Comic Book
16) DIY Comic Book Part II
17) Economic Collapse Survival Manual
18) Find The Ideal Husband
19) Football Play Design Book
20) Freakshow Los Angeles
21) Game Creation Manual
22) George Washington's Farewell Address
23) Hagakure
24) History of Aliens
25) Hollywood Talent Agency Directory
26) I Dream in Haiku
27) Internet Connected World
28) Irish Republican Army Manual of

Guerrilla Warfare

29) Japan History Coloring Book

30) John Locke's 2nd Treatise on Civil Government

31) Karate 360

32) Learning Magic

33) Living the Pirate Code

34) Magic as Science and Religion

35) Magicians Coloring Book

36) Make Racists Afraid Again

37) Master Password Organizer Handbook

38) Mikazuki Jujitsu Manual

39) Mikazuki Political Science Manual

40) MMA Coloring Book

41) Mythology Coloring Book

42) Mythology Dictionary

43) Native Americana

44) Ninja Style

45) Ouija Board Enigma

46) Palloncino

47) Political Advertising Manual

48) Quotes Gone Wild

49) Rappers Rhyme Book

50) Saving America

51) Self-Examination Diary

52) Shinzen Karate

53) Shogun X the Last Immortal

54) Small Arms & Deep Pockets

55) Stories of a Street Performer

56) Storyboard Book

AMERICAN BOOKSTORE
DIRECTORY

Facebook.com/MikazukiPublishingHouse

AMERICAN BOOKSTORE
DIRECTORY

KAMBIZ MOSTOFIZADEH TITLES
1. 25 Principles of Martial Arts
2. 25 Principles of Strategy
3. American Antifa
4. American Bookstore Directory
5. Arctic Black Gold
6. Back To Gold
7. Camping Survival Handbook
8. Economic Collapse Survival Manual
9. Find the Ideal Husband
10. Game Creation Manual
11. History of Aliens
12. Hollywood Talent Agency Directory
13. Internet Connected World
14. Karate 360
15. Learning Magic
16. Magic as Science & Religion
17. Make Racists Afraid Again
18. Mikazuki Jujitsu Manual
19. Mikazuki Political Science Manual
20. Mythology Dictionary
21. Native Americana
22. Ninja Style
23. Ouija Board Enigma
24. Political Advertising Manual
25. Saving America
26. Small Arms & Deep Pockets
27. Shinzen Karate
28. The Bribe Vibe
29. Van Carlton Detective Agency: Burgundy Diamond

AMERICAN BOOKSTORE
DIRECTORY

30.   World War Water
Facebook.com/KambizMostofizadeh

If the Mikazuki Publishing House™ book is not available place a request with any bookstore to order it for you.

Mikazuki Publishing House™ is a book

publisher that started in 2011 in Los Angeles

California. The Mikazuki Publishing House™ .

Trademark is protected by the United States

Patent Trade Organization Trademark

Registration Number 4323734.